To Lindsey & Doris[...]

Now that L[...]

of leisure he wi[...]

plenty of time to try all

these delicious dishes.

Merry Christmas

Travis & Carolyn

1991

The FAT WHITE GUY'S COOKBOOK

LUDLOW PORCH
AND
DIANE COX PORCH

LONGSTREET PRESS
Atlanta, Georgia

Published by
LONGSTREET PRESS
2150 Newmarket Parkway
Suite 102
Marietta, Georgia 30067

Printed in the United States of America

1st printing, 1990

Library of Congress Catalog Card Number: 90-061849

ISBN 0-929264-76-2

This book was printed by R. R. Donnelley & Sons, Harrisonburg,
Virginia. The text was set in Century Expanded by Typo-Repro
Service, Inc., Atlanta, Georgia.
Book design by Paulette Livers Lambert

For Ludlow, who sometimes eats white asparagus when he'd rather be eating white beans.

—D.C.P

For Diane, who sometimes insists I eat white asparagus when I'd rather be eating white beans.

—L.P.

ACKNOWLEDGMENTS

We'd like to thank all of the talented cooks in our lives who share their hospitality and recipes so generously.

And special thanks to Deborah Woolley-Lindsay who makes dreams come true.

CONTENTS

FOREWORD

When I was first asked to co-author a cookbook, I was reluctant. I thought, "Who am I to be writing a cookbook?" Then I thought, "I'm married to the best cook in the world. My mother was one of the finest Southern cooks ever to fry a chicken, as was my Grandmother."

In addition to my Southern lineage, I happen to know as much about eating as anybody that ever lived. I don't like to brag, but compared to me, Henry VIII was a health food nut. The fact of the matter is, I know more about eating than Edison knew about a 40 watt bulb.

With Diane telling you how to cook, and me telling you how to eat, this could be a fun project.

Diane has a much broader knowledge of food than I do. She is a true expert on food, all food, and cooking from Chinese to French; from German to Snellville.

On the other hand, my favorite foods in the world are the dishes from the deep South.

When I cook breakfast, my favorite is what I call my all-white meal.

I fry two eggs, I fix cathead biscuits (we call them that because they're as big as a cat's head). I fix a big bowl of milky gravy to spoon over the catheads. I fry fatback, and fix a big pot of grits. If you put this all on a white plate and then put the plate on a white tablecloth, you will find that your breakfast is not only delicious, it is dang near invisible. If you would like to add a little color to my all white meal, you can do so by adding loads of black pepper to the biscuits and gravy. If this is not enough color, you can put a dob of cow butter in the middle of your grits.

If you don't know what a dob of cow butter is, you would, in all likelihood, not enjoy this breakfast anyway, and I recommend you try "The International House of Oat Bran."

I don't want to leave the impression that I eat only food that is white . . . that is not true at all. But, I would be less than honest if I didn't tell you that I could get by quite nicely eating only white food. Some of my favorites are mashed potatoes, white bread, onions, rice and gravy, the white meat of chicken, biscuits, coconut cake, banana pudding, buttermilk, navy beans, coleslaw . . . get the idea?

I don't think you have to be born in the South to know about good eating, but I'm convinced it gives you a headstart. Some of my earliest memories about good eating were from what we called "all day singing and dinner on the grounds." I didn't care a lot about singing in church all day, but the eating was something else again. This wonderful happening always came on Sunday after preachin'. The ladies of the congregation would all bring food . . . lots and lots of food. I don't know if it was some kind of rule or not, but the food there was always Southern and always wonderful. It was not uncommon at all for the dinner table to be a hundred feet long with every inch of it being covered with platter after platter of golden brown fried chicken, five or six hams, every kind of bean on the planet, creamed corn, fried corn, corn on the cob, sliced tomatoes, stacks of rolls, cornbread, white loaf bread, row after row of casseroles and at least one large dish pan of barbecue pig.

The desserts were enough to give diabetes to a tree. Cakes, pies, rice pudding, banana pudding, egg custard and sometimes even homemade ice cream.

When you had worked your way to the end of the table, you found on the ground a number-three wash tub full of sweet iced tea.

It was always great fun to be there and try to count the number of people who never came to church except for the all day singing and dinner on the grounds. I don't guess anybody ever went to Heaven because of them, but I betcha a lot of folks went to Weight Watchers.

We always seemed to eat better at our house when we had company. My grandmother and grandfather were both from the Carolinas and about twice a year, we would have relatives come through town. In those days, nobody called long distance unless it was a genuine life-or-death emergency.

The relatives would call from the north side of town to tell us they would be there in about an hour. My grandmother would spring into action. She gave everybody in the house a job. It had to be done fast cause "company was coming"— that was the rallying cry—and everybody set about sweeping the floors, snapping the beans and shelling the peas. My grandmother would put about two handfuls of chicken feed in her apron. She would go to our chicken lot and start to sprinkle the feed around her feet. The whole time she was saying in a low, soft voice, "chick . . . chick . . . chick-a-baby . . . chick . . . chick . . . chick-a-baby." When a trusting chicken got close enough, Mama would move like lightning, grab the clucking bird by the neck and, in one motion, ring his neck. While her first victim was flapping around on the ground, Mama was going, "chick . . . chick . . . chick-a-baby" while she sprinkled the chicken feed. In a matter of seconds, she had three or four chickens ready to be dunked into the scalding hot water.

By the time our Carolina company arrived, the house was clean as a Bible verse, the front porch had been scrubbed down, and supper was almost ready.

Supper, in addition to mounds of fried chicken, included one other meat, five or six vegetables, cornbread, rolls, iced tea and a dessert.

One of the relatives would usually say to my grandmother, "Bessie, you sure do set a nice table." My grandmother would say, "I just wish I had known you all were coming so I could have fixed you something nice."

The entire purpose of this cookbook is to help you set a nice table.

BREAKFAST

I know that breakfast is supposed to be the most important meal of the day. Every doctor on the face of the earth will tell you that the biggest meal should be breakfast. They are unable, however, to tell you how this is possible. In the mornings I am always on wide open and never seem to have the time to sit down for a big meal. The weekends, however, are something else. I love to sleep late on weekends and wake up to one of my Diane's delicious meals. Read on . . .

Saturday Breakfast

Lud usually has four or five patties of sausage (with mustard) and coffee on weekday mornings. He eats while he drives to work.

I have cereal.

Weekend breakfasts are a big production, though: Bo Whaley brings us the most fabulous hot sausage from Dublin, Georgia, and I keep it in the freezer at the cabin. (Lud has commercial sausage during the week—Bo's sausage is too special for "everyday.") I scramble eggs with cheese in them, make cathead biscuits with gravy, slice home grown tomatoes (or cantelope in winter), cook a pot of grits and squeeze fresh juice. There must be enough cholesterol there to clog every artery between Dawsonville and the cardiac ICU at Emory.

The recipes in this chapter aren't for the standard breakfast. Like Bo's sausage, they're special.

 # Sunday Scrambled Eggs

6 eggs
1¹/₂ slices of Old English cheese
¹/₂ teaspoon garlic powder
tiny sprinkle of onion powder
1 tablespoon chopped parsley
a dribble of milk
salt and pepper
bacon grease

Put the eggs, garlic powder, onion powder, milk, parsley, salt and pepper in a bowl and scramble. Break the cheese into small pieces and drop in. Coat the skillet with bacon grease and cook the egg mixture very slowly. This isn't much extra work and makes a world of difference.

 # Easy Brunch Egg Casserole

In the bottom of a greased 1½-quart baking dish, combine 2 cups seasoned croutons and 1 cup each sharp Cheddar cheese and Swiss cheese. Combine 4 slightly beaten eggs, 2 cups milk, ½ teaspoon salt, ½ teaspoon prepared mustard, ⅛ teaspoon onion powder and ⅛ teaspoon pepper. Mix until blended and pour over the croutons and mix. Top with baconettes. Bake at 325 degrees for 55 to 60 minutes. This can be done the day before.

Slightly Harder Brunch Egg Casserole

¹/₄ cup butter
¹/₄ cup flour
2 cups milk
1¹/₂ dozen hard boiled eggs, sliced
¹/₄ teaspoon thyme
¹/₄ teaspoon majoram
¹/₄ teaspoon basil
1 pound grated sharp Cheddar cheese
¹/₄ cup parsley
buttered bread crumbs
1 package chipped, dried beef

Make a sauce of the butter, flour and milk over low heat. Add the herbs, cheese and beef, stirring until the cheese melts. Layer in a baking dish, sliced eggs, parsley, and a third of the sauce; repeat twice. Top with bread crumbs and bake at 350 degrees for 30 minutes. This one, too, can be made ahead.

Breakfast Casserole

This one's great for overnight guests!

6 slices bread, blended into crumbs
6 eggs

2 cups milk
1 pound sausage, browned and drained
1 cup Cheddar cheese, shredded
salt and pepper to taste

Mix eggs, milk, salt and pepper. Line a 1½-quart casserole dish with bread crumbs. Put cooked sausage on top of the bread crumbs. Cheese goes on top of the sausage. Pour the egg mixture over all. Refrigerate overnight. Bake at 350 degrees for 45 minutes.

 # Shirred Eggs with Bacon

This is *not* a pretty dish, but the taste makes up for it! I make this in individual ramekins when I need more or less of it. Adults love it. Give the kids cereal.

4 slices Canadian bacon
2 thin slices Swiss cheese, cut into two pieces.
4 eggs
½ teaspoon salt
¼ teaspoon white pepper
¼ cup dairy sour cream

Preheat the oven to 400 degrees. Place the bacon in the bottom of an 8-inch pie plate. Place slices of cheese over the bacon. Break the eggs on top of the cheese. Mix up the salt, pepper and sour cream and spoon it over the top of the eggs. You can sprinkle chopped chives over the whole thing, if you want. Bake it for 15 to 20 minutes, or until the whites of the eggs are set. Makes 4 servings.

—

 Country Ham

Most folks will tell you they don't like country ham because it's too salty. Indeed it is, unless you wash it first.

I just rinse it off so it's still quite salty. Some folks soak it for 15 minutes or so.

Also make sure the ham is sliced thin. Country ham is tough and if it's thick sliced, you can't chew it at all.

With biscuits and red-eye gravy, you've got breakfast.

Ludlow's Grits Grizzard

Grits Grizzard is one of my favorite ways to fix grits. Like most great contributions to mankind, Grits Grizzard was born after countless hours of experimentation. This dish was born in my kitchen about 4:30 A.M. Lewis and I had been celebrating Michigan Arbor Day. We had each consumed several adult beverages and along about daylight, we decided to prepare breakfast.

When the pot of grits was almost ready, Lewis put some grated cheese into the bubbling white wonderfulness. We tasted the dish and agreed that it was wonderful, but it needed something.

Lewis said, "Do you know what's wrong with this pot of grits? I'll tell you what's wrong . . . They're not greasy enough. Everybody knows that grease makes everything better."

There was a frying pan of fresh sausage grease on the stove. Lewis put 3 or 4 spoonfuls of the sausage grease into the grits. We put a serving on our plates, a big dob of butter in the middle, lots of black pepper . . . and Grits Grizzard was born.

Cheese Grits

Even yankees who don't like grits will go for this.

3 cups water
³/₄ cup uncooked regular grits
¹/₄ teaspoon salt
¹/₈ teaspoon garlic powder
1¹/₂ cups (6 ounces) shredded sharp Cheddar cheese
¹/₈ teaspoon hot sauce
¹/₃ cup egg substitute, or one egg slightly beaten
vegetable cooking spray

Bring water to a boil in a medium saucepan and add grits. Cover, reduce heat and simmer 10 minutes. Add salt and next three ingredients, stirring until the cheese melts. Stir a small amount of hot grits into the egg substitute; then add remaining grits, stirring constantly. Pour the mixture into a 1-quart baking dish coated with cooking spray. Bake at 350 degrees for 40 minutes or until the grits have set. Serves 6.

Ludlow's S.O.S.

Make a white sauce using 2 tablespoons melted butter. Add 2 tablespoons flour and cook one minute, stirring constantly. Slowly add two cups of milk (less if you like it thicker, more if you like it thinner). Open a small jar of Armour dried beef. Chop coarsely. Add to the white sauce with plenty of pepper. Serve over toast or biscuits.

If you're a veteran, or if you know a veteran, you know about S.O.S. It's been a mainstay in every American mess hall longer than anybody can remember.

In the military everybody complained about S.O.S., but everybody took seconds.

This is an easy recipe, and will turn out even better if the cook has a tatoo that says, "Death Before Dishonor."

SANDWICHES & SALADS

I guess the reason I am so fond of sandwiches is that to make one, you start with two of my favorite things: white bread and mayonnaise. From that point, you let your imagination and your creativity take over.

A sandwich is a little like life . . . you put good things into it and you got yourself a winner. You can have a real treat if you keep an open mind and remember that you can make a sandwich out of almost anything.

One of my favorites is fresh white Colonial bread, mayonnaise and my famous French fries. That's right, a French fry sandwich. Nothing fancy, just delicious. Same with an onion sandwich: sliced Vidalia onion, mayonnaise and bread.

Ah yes, the sandwich, the last bastion of creativity for the glutton who is not much of a cook.

Classic Banana Sandwich

Remember this one?

> *2 slices Colonial bread*
> *1 banana*
> *mayonnaise*

Mayonnaise the bread and peel the banana.

I suggest slicing the banana into neat circles horizontally and lining them up on the bread, overlapping slightly. (Lettuce is wonderful on this sandwich.)

Ludlow, on the other hand, prefers the banana sliced vertically—which produces a somewhat uneven amount of banana in the mouth. (He's also trying to get an Anti-Lettuce-on-Banana-Sandwiches Law through the legislature.)

 # Peanut Butter & Banana Sandwich

Same as Classic Banana Sandwich except one slice of bread is covered thickly with peanut butter and the other with mayonnaise.

Classic Pineapple Sandwich

Prepare according to directions for Classic Banana Sandwich, using pineapple rings instead of banana. How you make it fit is entirely up to you.

 # THE Grilled Cheese Sandwich

2 slices Colonial bread
1 slice Kraft Old English cheese
butter or margarine

Butter one side of each slice of bread. Put the cheese between the slices with the butter on the *outside* of the sandwich. Put in a small skillet. Cover and cook on medium-low heat. When it's perfectly golden on the bottom, flip it over and cook the other side.

Add cooked bacon and a slice of home-grown tomato before grilling, if you have some company you want to impress.

Pita Pocket Sandwich

1 Pita round
2 slices ham
2 slices Swiss cheese
Thousand Island dressing
Vidalia onion
a dob of cow butter

Slice the pita in half to form two pockets. Coat the inside of each with Thousand Island dressing. Saute Vidalia onion rings in the butter, slightly. Move onion to the side of skillet. Put in the ham. Turn the ham and place cheese and onion atop the ham. Cover a few seconds to let the cheese melt. Fold the ham over and slip into the pita pocket.

 # Ludlow's Sink Sandwich

The main ingredient in a sink sandwich can be anything from ham to fried egg.

Make your favorite sandwich using an excessive amount of mayonnaise. For a *true* sink sandwich you must have a slice of red, ripe, juicy, homegrown tomato. Make that two slices.

This sandwich should only be eaten if you're wearing a short-sleeved shirt. If the tomato is ripe enough, the juice will run down to your elbows.

Always stand over the kitchen sink and eat as rapidly as possible. This will save you countless thousands of dollars on your dry cleaning bills.

If you are a true sink sandwich connoisseur, it is perfectly proper to make soft, low moaning sounds during the few seconds it will take to devour this delicacy.

Back in the 50's Mama would put two or three lettuce leaves on the salad plate, arrange two pineapple rings on them, and put a dob of mayonnaise in the pineapple hole. Then she'd put a cherry on each mayonnaise blob. I made it for Luddy a few weeks ago. Turned out his mom made the same thing. Lord, how I love old recipes.

Another one my mom did was pears stuffed with cream cheese and chopped pecans mashed together, and stuffed into the hollow of the pear. She'd put the pears, stuffing side down, in an individual mold and pour lime Jell-O over it. When it was cold and unmolded it looked like a jewel.

Remember canned pears on lettuce with mayonnaise in the hollow, grated cheese sprinkled over it and a cherry on top?

Precious memories, how they linger. (—Diane)

 ## Avocado Salad

I never liked avocados until Debbie Harris served us this.

(I still don't like avocado, Debbie Harris notwithstanding. —Ludlow)

1 cubed, ripe avocado
1/2 chopped onion
mayonnaise to moisten
seasoned salt

Just mix it all up, chill and enjoy. (Wouldn't it be good with some small, boiled shrimp thrown in?)

Buttermilk Salad

1 6-ounce package peach-flavored gelatin
3 tablespoons sugar
1 8¹/₂-ounce can of crushed pineapple, undrained
2 cups buttermilk
1 10-ounce carton non-dairy whipped topping
¹/₂ cup chopped pecans

Place the first three ingredients in a small pan, and stir over low heat until melted. Allow to cool. Add two cups of buttermilk and the whipped topping. Mix with beater. Stir-in chopped pecans. Spoon into a 9-by-9 square pan. Chill until firm. Cut into squares and serve on lettuce leaves.

Hint for weight watchers: use a sugar substitute and pineapple canned in its own juices.

 # Hot Chicken Salad

4 whole chicken breasts, cooked
4 hard-cooked eggs
¹/₂ can cream of chicken soup
2 cups celery, finely chopped
¹/₃ cup mayonnaise
1 cup sour cream
1 8-ounce can sliced water chestnuts, drained
1 4-ounce can mushrooms
¹/₃ cup slivered almonds
2 tablespoons minced onions

2 tablespoons lemon juice
dash of pepper
1 teaspoon salt
1 cup grated sharp cheddar cheese
1 3¹/₂ ounce can onion rings

Cut the cooked chicken into one-inch pieces. Mix chicken with the remaining ingredients, except cheese and onion rings. Place in a 13″ × 9″ inch casserole. Top with the cheese and bake at 350 degrees for 30 minutes. Remove and sprinkle with the onion rings and bake 15 minutes longer. Serves six.

W.D. Crowley's
Hunt Club Dogwood Salad

Romaine lettuce leaves
1 cantaloupe, peeled and quartered
1 honeydew melon, peeled and quartered
1 pound king crab meat, diced
4 teaspoons Dijon mustard
1 cup mayonnaise
1 teaspoon vanilla
1 to 2 teaspoons Half & Half, enough to thin dressing
4 sprigs fresh parsley

Wash and trim Romaine leaves and arrange on each of four 9-inch plates. Cut quartered melons into thin slices, using a quarter of each melon per serving; alternate cantaloupe and honeydew, arranging clockwise on lettuce leaves. Place crab meat in the center of the plate. In a small bowl, combine mustard, mayonnaise and vanilla; thin with Half & Half as necessary. Spoon a ribbon of sauce over crab meat and garnish with parsley sprigs. Makes four servings.

Herbed Tomatoes

Of course, this is better with home-grown tomatoes, but if you ever manage to get any of those things the grocer calls tomatoes ripe this recipe will disguise them enough to make them edible. No small trick that!

6 ripe tomatoes, peeled and sliced
1 teaspoon salt
¼ teaspoon freshly ground pepper
½ teaspoon dried thyme or marjoram, crushed
¼ cup finely snipped parsley
¼ cup snipped chives
⅔ cup salad oil
¼ cup tarragon vinegar

Place tomatoes in a bowl. Sprinkle with seasonings and herbs. Combine oil and vinegar, pour over. Cover and chill 3 hours, spooning dressing over tomatoes a few times. Drain off the dressing and serve.

 # Lentil Salad

1½ cups dried lentils
¾ cup olive oil
⅓ to ½ cup balsamic vinegar
½ cup chopped fresh parsley
¼ cup soy sauce
½ teaspoon hot sauce or more to taste
garlic salt to taste

2 cups chopped celery
¹/₂ cup chopped Vidalia onion
salad greens and tomato wedges

Place lentils in large saucepan with 4 cups water, hot sauce, and soy sauce. Bring to boil, reduce heat, and simmer covered about 30 to 40 minutes, until lentils are tender. You may have to add a bit more water if the lentils absorb all of the 4 cups initially used. Add oil, vinegar, and the parsley. Mix well and cool. Add garlic salt. Stir in celery and onion. Cover and chill for several hours. Turn into a bowl lined with greens and garnished with tomato.

 # Diane's Potato Salad

Potato Salad is so personal that it probably shouldn't be in a book. My recipe was my mother's. I added celery seed and garlic powder to it, but basically it's the same.

Boil, covered, whole washed potatoes with their jackets on. They're done when a paring knife can be inserted easily. (If the center is even slightly hard, your potato salad is going to taste like raw potato.) Cool, peel and dice. Add chopped onion and celery, diced pimento and pickle relish that has been drained well ... squeeze it in paper towels. Sprinkle with salt and pepper (celery seed and garlic powder are optional).

Toss with just barely enough Kraft mayonnaise to moisten. Add a tad of yellow mustard and stir gently. Refrigerate a couple of hours ... it's even better the next day.

Paul Sachetti's Potato Salad

This is a nice change from my plain old potato salad, and it's prettier:

> *new potatoes boiled in the skin and quartered*
> *frozen pea pods, steamed for 30 seconds*
> *red bell pepper, chopped or sliced in rings*
> *salt*
> *pepper*
> *dill, lots!*
> *sour cream*

Just chill ingredients, and mix with enough sour cream to moisten.

 ## Shrimp Salad

> *boiled, cleaned shrimp cut into grape sized pieces*
> *about half as much chopped celery as you have*
>   *shrimp*
> *mayonnaise to moisten*
> *1 teaspoon lemon juice*

Mix together and chill. You may never want chicken salad again.

Special Spinach Salad

1 pound fresh spinach
1 can French-fried onion rings
8 slices fried bacon
3 hard-cooked eggs
1 tablespoon Worcestershire sauce
2 tablespoons salad oil
1/2 cup sugar
1/3 cup ketchup
1 small onion, grated
1/4 cup brown cider vinegar

Clean and dry spinach. Add onion rings, crumbled bacon, and chopped eggs to spinach. Toss. Combine the remaining ingredients and heat to a boil. Pour over the spinach mixture. Toss and serve immediately.

 # Taco Salad

One of the Porch clan brought this taco salad to a family reunion. I wanted to eat all of it, but she wouldn't let me. Instead, she gave me the recipe. (And now, I can't remember her name — a relative too! I wish I were dead.)

1 onion, chopped
1 15-ounce can kidney beans, drained and minced
1 ripe avocado, chopped

½ cup shredded Cheddar cheese
3 tomatoes, chopped
3 ounces sliced ripe olives
8 ounces Catalina dressing (lite is fine)

Mix ingredients and chill. Before serving, toss with ½ head of torn lettuce and 4-6 cups of corn chips.

 # Waldorf Salad

2 cups diced apples
1 cup chopped celery
½ cup pecans
½ cup raisins
1 cup grapes
1 sliced banana
juice of 1 lemon
mayonnaise

Toss apples and bananas with lemon juice to prevent discoloration. Add all the other ingredients, mixing mayonnaise to moisten. Serves 8.

VEGETABLES

In all truthfulness, I probably know a great deal more about eating vegetables than cooking them. I do know one thing, however: vegetables should be cooked to death.

A pole bean is just about done when it starts to turn a little black. One of the most repulsive sights in the world is a brightly colored pole bean on my plate. This usually happens up north or in a hotel dining room. Not only is it ugly, it tastes like a fan belt.

It's okay for a breakfast cereal to go "snap," "crackle" and "pop," but a pole bean should go squish when you bite into it.

Use a ham hock in cooking pole beans, unless you're poor, then use fatback. If your budget won't stand the fatback, you had better stop fooling with this cookbook and go find a job.

Nancy McAnally's Baked Beans

Drain a big can of pork and beans. Pick out that horrible little square of pork. Pour the beans in a big mixing bowl. Put about two blubs of catsup in and about the same amount of mustard. Add a half cup or so of brown sugar and stir. Taste it. You might like more sugar and mustard. Pour into a baking dish. Cut an onion into thin rings. Cover the top of the beans with onions. Lay strips of raw bacon side by side, touching, over the onion. Bake at 350 to 400 degrees until the bacon is crispy.

 # Green Beans Italian (Microwave)

3 slices bacon
2 10-ounce packages frozen green beans
¼ cup water
1 small onion
¾ cup bottled Italian dressing

Cook bacon. Put beans in a 1½-quart casserole dish. Add water. Cook covered on High for 9 minutes, stirring once. Add onion and dressing. Cook covered on High 4 minutes more. Let stand 3 minutes. Sprinkle with cooked bacon.

Aunt Barbara's Corn Pudding

When you see Barbara Cox's name on a recipe in this book, you can be sure it's great. She's my aunt and I've never had a mouthful at her table that wasn't scrumptious. This is Luddy's favorite corn recipe in the world:

> *1 medium can cream-style corn*
> *2 eggs well beaten*
> *2-3 tablespoons flour, or cornstarch*
> *1 tablespoon sugar*
> *several pats of butter to place on top*

Grease a 1-quart baking dish. Mix all ingredients together and pour in the dish. Cook at 350 degrees until firm, about 45 minutes to an hour.

 # Diane's Fried Okra

I don't believe anyone else fries okra the way I do; and quite frankly, the world's probably a better place because they don't. When I finish frying okra, no vitamin or mineral could've possibly lived through it. It's just crunchy grease, but it's wonderful.

Cut fresh okra thin. Make more than you think you'll need because it shrinks while you cook it. Melt ½ stick of butter in your iron skillet. (At least you may get a little iron!) Put the okras in. Salt it. Fry on medium high and stir from time to time. Don't take it out when it looks done. Fry it some more. When it's brown and crunchy, it's done. Drain, salt some more, and serve.

(This is a shonuff different way to fix fried okra. I was raised on okra that was battered and fried and I still love it that way. Don't expect this to taste anything like that. It's different, but makes a nice change. If you don't tell the kids what this is, they'll love it too. — Ludlow)

 # Ohmigod Potatoes

I got back to the cabin from running errands later than I expected. Lud and I were starving. He got the steaks out, seasoned them and put them on the grill. Meanwhile, I washed a big baking potato, stabbed it a few times and microwaved it until it was done. I sliced it, skin and all, into a small pyrex dish with a cover. I sprinkled a little salt and pepper on it and then made a white sauce. (Melt 1 tablespoon butter, add 1 tablespoon flour and stir and cook 1 minute. Slowly add 1 cup milk.) I found some chopped onion and bell pepper in the refrigerator and put it over the potatoes. It still looked pretty dull, so I sliced a tomato over the top. I poured the white sauce on top. (It didn't look like enough, but it was.) Since the dish was beginning to look good, I decided to garnish it with a slice of Old English cheese. I cut it into triangles and placed it carefully, making a darling geometric design. I put the lid on it and baked it until the steaks were done, 350 degrees for 15-20 minutes. The cheese disappeared down into the sauce, so you may as well just break it up. And it could stand more salt and pepper. But, Lawd, it was good!

Twice Baked Potatoes

2 big baking potatoes
¹/₂ stick of butter
¹/₂ cup sour cream
2 tablespoons chives
4 slices Old English cheese
salt and pepper
garlic powder
1 tablespoon minced onion (optional)
4 slices bacon, cooked (optional)

Stab the clean potatoes several times each. Don't wrap them in foil. (They won't be flaky if you do.) Don't grease the skins; you *want* them hard. Bake them.

When they're done, cut them in half and scoop the potato into a bowl. Add everything except the cheese and bacon. Taste and adjust the recipe to your liking. Top with cheese and put in the oven till the cheese melts. Sprinkle with bacon. You'll have to mash it in a little because it won't stick. Serves 4.

 # DeGraauw's Spinach Artichoke Casserole

3 packages frozen spinach, cooked
1 onion, chopped and sauteed in 1 stick of butter
¹/₃ cup fresh grated Parmesan cheese
1 cup sour cream
salt and pepper
plenty of garlic powder
2 cans artichoke hearts, drained and washed

Pour cooked spinach and sauteed onion into a big bowl and add remaining ingredients. Fold gently together and taste ... more garlic? Pour into a baking dish. Top with seasoned bread crumbs and drizzle with melted butter. Bake at 350 degrees until bubbly, 30-45 minutes.

Aunt Barbara's Squash Casserole

1 package Pepperidge Farm stuffing mix
1 stick oleo
2¹/₂ pounds squash, sliced and cooked
2 carrots, shredded
2 medium onions, chopped
8 ounces sour cream
1 can cream of chicken soup

Combine soup, sour cream, squash, carrots and onions. Melt oleo and mix with stuffing mix. Put ³/₄ of the stuffing mix in the bottom of a 4-quart baking dish. Put combined ingredients in next. Put the remainder of the stuffing mix on the top. Bake at 350 degrees for 20-30 minutes.

Sweet Potato Pie

¹/₂ cup whipping cream
1 teaspoon vinegar
1 teaspoon soda
2 cups cooked, mashed sweet potatoes
3 tablespoons butter, melted
1 cup sugar
1 teaspoon baking powder
¹/₂ teaspoon ground cinnamon
¹/₂ teaspoon ground nutmeg
3 eggs, beaten
1 unbaked 9-inch pastry shell

Combine whipping cream, vinegar and soda; stir well. Set aside. Combine the next 7 ingredients, mixing well. Stir into whipping cream mixture. Blend with an electric mixer till smooth. Pour filling into pastry shell. Bake at 400 degrees for 10 minutes, then reduce heat to 300 degrees. Bake 45-50 minutes. Serve hot or cold. Garnish pie with dollops of whipped cream and sprinkle with cinnamon if desired.

 # Ludlow's Homegrown Tomatoes

Peel, slice, and eat.
When tomatoes are in season, they should be eaten three meals a day ... everyday.

Hot Green Tomatoes

½ cup bias-sliced celery
3 green onions sliced into 1 inch pieces
2 tablespoons olive oil
1 clove garlic, crushed
⅛ teaspoon crushed red pepper
3 medium green tomatoes, each cut into 6 wedges
1 tablespoon fresh cilantro or parsley
fresh or pickled red hot pepper (optional, but be
  brave)

In a small microwave-safe bowl, combine celery, onion, olive oil, garlic and crushed red pepper. Microwave, covered, on 100% power for 1½ minutes. Arrange tomato wedges in a shallow 1 to 1½-quart microwave-safe dish. Spoon the onion mixture over the tomatoes. Sprinkle cilantro over all of it. Cook covered in the microwave at 100% power for 2½ to 4 minutes, or until tomatoes are fork tender and heated through, rotating the dish halfway through the cooking. Season with salt and pepper to taste and garnish with red hot pepper. Makes 4 servings.

Turnip Greens

I never *could* fix good turnip greens. I tried cooking them with ham hock, ham bones, smoked ham hock, bacon grease, butter, different seasonings—everything I could think of. I just couldn't make them taste like my mother's.

Several years ago we had dinner at Mel and Margaret Finkel's house and her turnip greens were perfect. I asked for her recipe and she said, "There's no recipe. All in the world I do is cook them with fatback and salt."

I'd put my turnip greens up against anybody's now.

SUPPER

Since TV came in in the early fifties, our language has just gone to Hell. Suddenly we all decided we should talk like Edward R. Murrow.

It happened almost overnight ... a davenport became a sofa, a parlor became a den, a "dope fiend" became a substance abuser and, God help us all, dinner became lunch, supper became dinner, and a late breakfast became brunch. I don't understand any of it. Let's talk about brunch. Can anyone tell me what time you stop having breakfast and start having brunch? Who decides? Is it what you eat or what time you eat it?

It's very confusing. When I was in school, we all went to the lunch room to have dinner. We knew by watching TV that while we were having supper, Lucy and Ricky and Fred and Ethel were having dinner. We didn't care because we had already had dinner while they were having lunch.

When the smoke had all cleared and we had accepted the fact that folks up north know best, here's what we wound up with: The morning meal was, of course, breakfast. The meal we eat in the middle of the day was lunch, and the evening meal was dinner. Supper was, by God, gone. Well, gang, let the record clearly show that at my house, we still eat supper every night. We eat breakfast every morning, and we eat dinner in the middle of the day.

I know what you're thinking . . . what about brunch? We eat brunch anytime we can come up with $17.50 for adults and $12.00 for children.

Diane's
Fried Chicken Supper

My Grandma always chose the young chickens to kill. She never went after the big mean ones that laid eggs and pecked me when I was sent to gather them. No, not her. She was after the young ones who had their whole lives ahead of them.

I was especially well behaved at Grandma's house.

Making fried chicken is easier now. You go to the store and buy five chicken breast halves. I skin them and clean them before I put them in the refrigerator. When I'm ready to use them, I take them out and wash them again. While they're still wet, I drop them individually into a plastic bag that has about 2 cups of flour, a few shakes of salt and a generous amount of pepper. I put the coated chicken on a platter and leave it alone for 30 or 45 minutes. Leaving it alone is probably the most important step. When I come back, the chicken looks like it's been dipped in wallpaper paste. That's going to make a crisp "skin" after it's fried. Then I put 2 to 3 inches of vegetable oil in my big iron skillet and heat it on medium high until it sizzles when a speck of flour drops in. I brown the chicken quickly on both sides. Always turn the chicken with tongs, never with a fork. If you don't pierce the breast, the juices stay in and the grease stays out. Finally, I turn the breasts meaty side down and cover the pan. Fry them slowly, covered, for 30 minutes. Drain on a paper towel.

While Lud sets the table and puts the food out, I make gravy. Pour off all but about 3 tablespoons of the fat from the chicken. Leave all those nice crunchy bits of flour in there. Return it to the heat and add 3 tablespoons of the flour you shook the chicken in. Add a good sprinkle of salt and stir and scrape for a minute. Slowly add milk, stirring and scraping constantly. It will take about 3 cups, depending on how thick you like your gravy. Add plenty of pepper and serve.

While the chicken is making its new "skin," I peel 15 potatoes, slice them thick and put them in a pot of cold water with a bit of salt. I cook them 30-40 minutes (until they break apart when I stick them with a fork). Then I drain them and put them back on the burner to dry all the water in the pan. I add about 1/4 cup of milk, 3 tablespoons of butter and a bit of salt and pepper, then mash them with a potato masher. (It's less trouble than the mixer and it reminds me of gentler times.)

I cook the pole beans the day before. I wash them and string them and break them into bite-sized pieces and cook them with a smoked ham hock. (The sooner Molly McButter comes out with Molly McHamhock, the better off we'll all be.) If the beans are those old, big ones from the grocer, they'll need to cook for over an hour. The good, fresh, small ones out of the garden don't take as long and taste infinitely better. (Salt them near the end of the cooking time.) I like to put them covered in the refrigerator overnight. They're tastier and I can lift the fat right off the top when it hardens ... if I'm feeling especially virtuous.

This supper contains enough calories for a fieldhand to plow the entire north forty with a lame mule.

Leftovers

Cold fried chicken is wonderful as it is. Any leftover mashed potatoes can be made into potato pancakes:

Add ½ chopped onion to the potatoes and a lightly beaten egg, several tablespoons of flour and enough milk to make the mixture look like thick, lumpy pancake batter. Add salt and pepper. Melt a tablespoon (maybe 2) of bacon grease in your iron skillet. Fry them in the same way you do pancakes.

Zap the pole beans in the microwave.

If there's leftover gravy, for Heaven's sake, throw it out!

After eating this way for two days running, it would be best to update your will and get right with the Lord.

Beef Stroganoff

I've lost my Beef Stroganoff recipe so Carl Proehl gave me his. I use fresh sauteed mushrooms and I don't put catsup in mine. Carl is one of the best cooks I know and I trust him, but, really, don't put catsup in it.

> *2 pounds round steak, cut in small cubes, or beef*
>   *sirloin*
> *1 large onion, diced*
> *¼ teaspoon garlic powder (optional)*
> *3 tablespoons soy sauce*
> *1 8-ounce can mushrooms (or fresh, sauteed)*
> *6 tablespoons catsup (questionable)*
> *4 tablespoons butter*

1 pint sour cream
3 tablespoons flour mixed in same amount of water
2 tablespoons dry white wine
salt, pepper, paprika to taste

Cook onion in butter until soft but not brown. Remove from pan with slotted spoon. Add meat to pan and saute until brown. Add onions, all seasonings, catsup and the juice from the can of mushrooms to the meat in pan and simmer at very low heat until the meat is tender. Add flour mixture to thicken and simmer a bit longer, then add mushrooms, sour cream and white wine. Cook slowly until heated thoroughly but do not boil! Serve over hot, buttered noodles or fluffy rice.

 # Brunswick Stew

2 hens
2 Boston butts
8 cans creamed style corn
8 cans tomatoes
4 bottles catsup
salt & pepper
4 cans tomato sauce
juice of 1 lemon
1 cup vinegar

Cook meat in a pressure cooker, salt and pepper to taste. Grind the meat and mix with remaining ingredients. Cook on low heat until thick, about 1 hour.

This is delicious, and it'll feed Coxey's army. But the fact of the matter is, if you're going to go to this much trouble you may as well drive on over to Harold's Barbeque and get the real thing. And they'll give you cracklin' cornbread with it.

Aunt Barbara's Chicken Breasts with Boursin

Take 12 boneless chicken breast halves and dredge in flour with salt and pepper. Layer each with 2 tablespoons boursin cheese, then a slice of proscuitto. Roll each and secure with a toothpick to close the ends. Brown them lightly in ¼ cup melted butter. Pour in 1 cup chicken stock and ½ cup Liquor Galliano. Cover and simmer about 30 minutes. Heat ⅓ cup of butter and ⅔ tablespoon Liquor Galliano. Add ½ pound sliced mushrooms and saute till tender. Add some coarsely chopped parsley and saute 3 minutes. Add to chicken before it's done. Serve with saffron rice or noodles.

 # Best-Ever Chicken

8 deboned chicken breasts
8 slices bacon
1 small jar dried beef
½ pint sour cream
1 can cream of mushroom soup

Line the bottom of the baking dish with dried beef. Wrap each breast with a slice of bacon. Place side by side in the dish on top of the beef. Mix the mushroom soup and sour cream and pour over chicken. Bake uncovered at 250 degrees for 3 hours. This can be prepared the day before.

Beverly Morgan, Judy Merritt and Miller Pope have given me this recipe at different times. Miller assured me that he's cooked it at higher temperatures for less time and had it turn out just fine. He also suggests mixing up some more sour cream and mushroom soup to pour over it 10-15 minutes before it comes out of the oven because so much of it evaporates.

Carl's Wild Rice & Chicken Livers

1 cup wild rice, washed and drained
3 cups boiling water
¹/₂ teaspoon salt
¹/₂ teaspoon Season-All
pinch of thyme
6 sprigs of fresh parsley, chopped
2 sprigs of celery leaves, chopped
2 bay leaves
1 medium onion, chopped
1 6-ounce can mushrooms
1 6-ounce can water chestnuts
4 tablespoons golden sherry
4 tablespoons soy sauce
black pepper
1 stick of butter

Place wild rice, salt, Season-All, thyme, parsley, celery, and the bay leaves into a pan containing the boiling water and simmer for fifty minutes or until rice is tender. Meanwhile, saute the onion, mushrooms, chestnuts, and the livers in the butter until the onions are light brown. When the rice is done, mix the liver mixture, the sherry, the soy sauce with the rice.

Pepper to taste. Pour into a casserole sprayed with Pam. Sprinkle with parmesan cheese, if you like, and bake uncovered for about thirty minutes at 375 degrees.

 # Teenie's Chicken Divan

4 or 5 chicken breast halves
1 package broccoli spears
2 cups Cheddar cheese, grated
1 can cream of celery soup
1 can cream of chicken soup
salt and pepper
slivered almonds

Boil chicken till tender and debone. Cook broccoli and drain. Mix soups together with salt and pepper. Layer ½ chicken, ½ broccoli and ⅓ cheese. Repeat the layers. Pour soup over all. Top with remaining cheese and slivered almonds. Bake at 350 degrees for 40 minutes.

 # Diane's Pullet Surprise

3 or 4 chicken breasts, skinned
1 cup uncooked rice
1 package Lipton onion soup mix

1 can mushroom soup
1¹/₂ cups chicken broth

Put the rice in the bottom of a buttered casserole. Sprinkle dry soup mix over rice. Spread half the mushroom soup and half the chicken broth over the rice and dry soup mix. Lay the chicken on top and pour the rest of the mushroom soup and broth over the top. Cook 2 hours, covered, at 325 degrees.

Dried Bean Supper

Wash the beans and pick out any with spots or discolorations. Cover them with four times as much water as you have beans. Throw out the floaters. Put a lid on the pot and soak them overnight.

Cook them in the water they soaked in with a ham hock, a whole onion, and a garlic clove. (I used to put a carrot and a rib of celery in, but I can't tell any difference without them.)

The time it takes to cook them varies. Navy beans are hard and take about three hours. Butter beans can get done in 30-45 minutes. Just taste them.

When they're done take out the garlic and onion and ham hock and whatever else you've put in there. Add salt and bring them back to a boil. Pepper them and put chopped raw onion on the top. Serve with cornbread, sliced homegrown tomatoes, green onions and buttermilk.

More power to you.

Quick Gazpacho

Major Peter's Bloody Mary mix
fresh tomatoes
cucumbers
bell pepper
onion
dill weed
pepper
sour cream

Chop all the vegetables. Put into Bloody Mary mix. Season with pepper and dill. Chill thoroughly. Serve with a dollop of sour cream on top.

 # Bruce Bartley's Ham Loaf

Bruce first served this to us about 10 years ago. The ham loaf is very good, but the sauce ... THE SAUCE!!! is what legends are made of. (Matter of fact, the sauce is great on prime rib.)

1¹/₂ pounds center cut raw ham, ground
³/₄ pound lean pork, ground
1 cup cracker crumbs
3 eggs
1 cup milk
salt and pepper to taste

Mix all ingredients together and put into a loaf pan. Bake at 325 degrees for 2 hours in a shallow pan of water.

SAUCE:

¹/₃ cup sugar
1 tablespoon dry mustard
¹/₄ teaspoon salt
¹/₃ cup mayonnaise
²/₃ cup sour cream
2 tablespoons coarsely ground horseradish

Mix the first three ingredients together well, add the last three and serve with the ham loaf.

Hungarian Goulash

My friend Nora is from Hungary. I called on her for this authentic recipe.

30 dkg marha- vagy sertéshús (esetleg vegyesen)
15 dkg leves-zöldség
50 dkg burgonya
hagyma
só
pirospaprika
csöves paprika
kö-ménymag
körömnyi babérlevél
2 evökanál olaj vagy
3 dkg zsir

Pörköltnek való húst veszünk, legjobb hozzá a pacsni, és két cm-es kockákra vágjuk. Az apróra vágott hagymát a zsiradékban fedö alatt megpiritjuk, beletesszük a pirospaprikát és hozzáadjuk a húst. Megsózzuk és vizzel felengedjük. Ha a hús puhulni kezd, megtisztítva és kettéhasítva tesszük bele a leveszöldséget. Amikor a hús majdnem készen van, hozzáadjuk a kockára vágott burgonyát és azzal lassú tüzön puhára fözzük. Nyáron zöldpaprikával, télen száraz csöves paprikával vagy lecsóval, illerve paprika- és paradicsomkrémmel, s tetszés szerint köménymaggal meg babérlevéllel izestijük.

 # Just Plain Meatloaf

1¹/₂ pounds lean ground round
1 egg, lightly beaten
1 onion, chopped
1-2 glugs of catsup
³/₄ cup wheat germ
several squirts of Worcestershire sauce
2 hefty sprinkles of Mrs. Dash
salt & pepper
garlic pepper
some bell pepper, chopped (if I have any)

I moosh all of it together with my hand then pack it into a glass loaf pan and bake it at 325 degrees until it "feels" done. Let me explain: After it cooks for thirty minutes or so, I take it out of the oven, hold a spatula over the top and pour off the grease. It's not done yet, so the spatula sinks down into the soft meat. Fifteen minutes later, I do it again. If it's still too soft I cook it some more. When it's done it's hard . . . but not real hard. Okay, poke a knife in the center, pull it back, and look in there. It's your meatloaf.

For an easy sauce, heat a small can of tomato sauce with a pinch of onion powder and a squirt of Worcestershire sauce. Pour it over the decanted meatloaf and serve.

 # Pepper Steak

3 tablespoons vegetable oil
¹/₄ cup minced onion
1 minced garlic clove
1 pound steak, tenderized and cut into 2 x ¹/₂ inch
  strips
1¹/₂ teaspoon kitchen bouquet
1 teaspoon salt
¹/₄ teaspoon pepper
2 green peppers cut into strips
1 teaspoon cornstarch
1 tablespoon dry vermouth

Saute onion in oil. Rub kitchen bouquet into meat. Brown the meat. Add spices. Cover and cook 8-10 minutes. Mix cornstarch and vermouth. Add to the meat mixture, and stir till sauce thickens. Add peppers, cover, and cook just long enough to wilt the peppers.

Pork Chops Supreme

4 large lean pork chops
8 lemon slices
8 Vidalia onion slices
brown sugar
catsup

Pre-heat oven to 350 degrees. Top each chop with two slices of lemon and onion. Sprinkle generously with brown sugar. Pour 1 tablespoon or so of catsup over each chop. Cover and bake for 1 hour, then uncover and bake for another 30 minutes. Baste occasionally.

 # Red Beans and Rice

Soak the dried beans overnight in 4 times as much water as you have beans. The next morning, put in a ham bone, a whole onion and several peeled garlic cloves. Cook the beans.

Meanwhile, cut smoked sausage into 3-inch pieces. Fry them in a covered skillet until browned. When the beans are nearly done, salt them. Take out the ham, onion and garlic. Add the sausage. Continue to cook until the beans are soft.

When they are done, mash some of the beans to thicken the soup. Serve over rice. Invite a Cajun.

(If you don't have any rice, try serving this one over cornbread; then it becomes "red beans and cornbread." Don't invite a Cajun, invite me. — Ludlow)

Ludlow's Red Hots

You can find "Red Hots" in the meat department of any grocery or convenience store. The name brand doesn't matter. Of all the great gourmet foods in the world, Red Hots are the easiest to prepare.

Slice the Red Hot down the middle, lengthwise; slice it almost, but not quite in two. Put the Red Hot into a hot, lightly greased frying pan and fry until the Red Hot is slightly burned.

Next, put mustard on two slices of Colonial white bread. Do not use any fancy, sissy gourmet mustard. Use plain old off-the-shelf-at-the-Piggly-Wiggly mustard.

If you eat two of these Red Hot sandwiches just before bedtime, in all likelihood, you will dream of living your life with Sam Donaldson in Patterson, New Jersey.

 # Salmon Croquettes

My grandmother made these when I was a little girl. I use some wheat germ to replace some of the soda cracker crumbs; otherwise, the recipe is the same.

My salmon croquettes are very good unadorned, and I ate them that way contentedly for forty years or so (even though Ludlow puts mustard on his).

But Marlene Sanders changed my life when she served them with Bearnaise sauce. Now, I can't imagine them without it.

53

2 small cans red or pink salmon
1 beaten egg
cracker crumbs and wheat germ
1 chopped celery rib
1 chopped onion
pepper

Pick over the salmon and get all the skin and little bones out. Save the liquid. Mix all the ingredients together, adding liquid and crumbs and wheat germ as needed to thicken enough for everything to stick together. Form into patties (like hamburgers) and fry in a little bacon grease until golden.

 # Ludlow's Shish Kebabs

I've never been able to fix shish kebab on the grill. I've ruined so much sirloin that I've quit trying.

My shish kebabs require a campfire. I learned how to make this one-dish dinner during my deer hunting days. It's quick, tasty, and there's very little clean-up.

In addition to your skewers, you'll need:

Sirloin steak
potatoes
firm, crunchy apples
onion

Cut everything into large bite-sized pieces. Alternate it on the skewer. Cook over an open campfire until the steak is done to suit your taste. Eat with white loaf bread.

Shrimp Moutard

Carl and Marilyn made this for us one night. Eight shrimp for each person is not enough. We wanted enough to swim in.

32 shrimp, steamed and shelled
1 cup mayonnaise
¹/₂ cup Dijon mustard
¹/₂ cup chopped Vidalia onion
¹/₂ cup chopped celery

Place 8 shrimp in each of four small baking dishes. Mix the mayonnaise, mustard, onion, and celery together. Spoon mixture over shrimp. Bake in a pre-heated oven at 425 degrees for 20 minutes or until the sauce is bubbly and slightly browned.

Turkey Stuffed Peppers

Ludlow couldn't tell these from the traditional recipe with ground beef!

³/₄ pound ground turkey
1 lightly beaten egg or Eggbeaters
6 soda crackers, crushed

55

3 tablespoons Heinz 57 sauce
3 tablespoons catsup
1/2 medium onion, chopped
1 teaspoon Mrs. Dash
2 large bell peppers

Mix the first seven ingredients well. Cut tops off bell peppers and clean out core and all seeds. Stuff the meat mixture into peppers. Bake at 350 degrees for 1 hour. After they brown, you may need to cover the tops with a small piece of aluminum foil to prevent burning.

FAMILY HOLIDAY FEAST

We always have the same old things for Thanksgiving and Christmas. Any variation is considered a sin against the family. Tradition is tradition, and I've come to accept it over the years. It's boring, but it's ours.

THE MENU

Turkey
Dressing
Easy Chicken Gravy
Cranberry Sauce
Holiday Congealed Salad
Creamed Peas
Holiday Sweet Potatoes
Mashed Potatoes
Ambrosia
Relish Tray
Refrigerator Rolls
Iced Tea

Turkey

Roasting tables and extensive directions for cooking turkeys are in most big cookbooks. I follow those directions except for a few things:

I don't put stuffing up the bird's ... cavity. After I wash it out good, I rub it with sage and put in a couple of quartered onions, a sliced carrot, a rib or two of celery, cut up, and an apple cut in several pieces. Nobody ever eats it, or even sees it, and I'm not sure it adds anything to the flavor of the meat. I just do it. (Old habits are hard to break.)

The best way I've found to cook a turkey isn't in any cookbook I've ever seen. I wrap the naked, clean bird in four or five layers of cheesecloth and pour melted oleo on the cheesecloth until it's completely soaked. I go back and baste it, but less frequently than I would without the cheesecloth. I bake it according to the roasting tables and take its temperature to be sure it's done. Then I cut and pull all the cheesecloth off. It looks burnt and horrible, but I don't panic because there's always a beautiful turkey underneath and it's never dried out or tough.

Dressing

Pepperidge Farm Seasoned Stuffing Mix
or
a big pan of cornbread
eggs
butter
chicken broth

celery
onion
mushrooms
sage
thyme
celery seed
garlic powder
salt and pepper

I used to bake cornbread for dressing. Once I tried the stuffing mix, I quit.

Measurements for dressing are pretty hopeless. It depends on how much you need to make and how you want it to taste. The first four ingredients are absolutely necessary, after that you're on your own.

I do it this way:

Dump two small bags or one big bag of stuffing in a big bowl. Add two beaten eggs and a stick and a half of butter. Add enough chicken stock to make it the way you like it. Dry, crumbly dressing doesn't take but 1 or 2 cups (or less) of stock. Wet dressing takes about 3. Keep stirring, and when it's the consistency of dressing your mama made, quit adding stock. Add 1 tablespoon sage, 2 teaspoons thyme, salt and pepper, a tablespoon or so of celery seed, 1 large chopped yellow onion and 5 ribs of celery (leaves and all). Saute ½ pound of mushrooms in a dob of cow butter. Cover. When the mushrooms give up some of their moisture, pour all of it in the dressing. Stir well. Put in a glass baking dish, cover with foil and bake at 350 degrees for 35 minutes. Uncover during the last 10 minutes of cooking.

Easy Chicken Gravy

Judy Merritt and her family were our guests at Thanksgiving one year. We were enjoying the pleasure of their company so much that I forgot to make the gravy for the turkey. Judy sent her husband, Bill, to the store for 2 cans of cream of chicken soup while she boiled 2 eggs. She heated those cans of soup, chopped the hard boiled eggs in it, thinned it with a tad of milk, and that was it.

That was over twenty years ago and I've used that recipe for every Thanksgiving and Christmas ever since.

But, if you want real chicken gravy, try this:

> *¹/₄ cup chicken fat*
> *¹/₄ cup flour*
> *1 cup chicken stock*
> *1¹/₂ cups milk*
> *a pinch of sage and thyme*
> *salt and pepper to taste*

Heat the fat, add flour and stir while it cooks 2 to 3 minutes. Slowly add chicken broth and milk. (Use more or less to determine thickness.) Add spices. To get a more "chickeny" taste, use a chicken bouillon cube or two.

Holiday Congealed Salad

1 package apple gelatin (the only place I've been able
    to find it is at Kroger under their own label)
2 diced red apples
3-4 ribs of celery, chopped
²/₃ package dates
³/₄ cup broken pecans

All you do is fill the mold with the mixed fruits and nuts, then cover with the gelatin to hold it together.

 # Creamed Peas

You'll like these creamed peas even if you don't like creamed peas. They're quick enough to make during a commercial and delicious with everything. They'll make your tongue beat your brains out. (— Ludlow)

1 large can tiny peas
1¹/₂ tablespoons butter
1¹/₂ tablespoons flour

Melt butter in a pot. Add the flour. Cook, stirring constantly, for 1 minute. Slowly add the liquid from the peas, stirring constantly. Put the peas in the sauce. Cover and heat on low.

Holiday Sweet Potatoes

4 cooked, mashed sweet potatoes
¹/₂ stick butter
¹/₂ cup brown sugar
1 teaspoon cinnamon
1 teaspoon nutmeg
a pinch of salt
juice of a juicy orange
miniature marshmallows (optional)

Mix it all with a mixer. Either put it in a casserole and bake, or for individual servings, hollow out 8-10 orange halves and cook the potatoes in the shells. Bake 20-30 minutes at whatever temperature the meat's on. If you like, you can put marshmallows on top during the last few minutes of baking.

 # Ambrosia

I don't like making ambrosia. Leaning over the sink and peeling oranges with the sticky juice running to my elbows and my nose invariably itching makes me miserable. Every year I swear I'm not going to do it. (There's already *enough*!) Every year the kids beg and finally offer to help. So, every Christmas, Leena, my oldest daughter and I stand over the sink, peeling oranges with our noses itching.

If you're bound to make ambrosia, here's the way to do it:

Buy two bags of Florida oranges, coconut — fresh or frozen or canned — and Maraschino cherry halves. Go home and eat one of the oranges. If it isn't sweet, go to another store and buy two more bags of oranges. (It doesn't happen often, only when you're rushed.)

Stand over the sink and peel the oranges deeply. Leave plenty of the meat on the skins to make sure there's not one tiny speck of the white inner peeling on the orange. Section the orange, making sure none of the membrane or seeds are left on the sections. Put the sections in a glass bowl. Squeeze the pulp into the bowl to get all the juice out. Run your thumb down the inside of the peeling to get the juice. Do that with everyone of those blasted oranges. Add enough coconut to make it look like ambrosia, add the drained cherry halves for color. Chill and serve.

If any member of your Christmas gathering doesn't act like he or she just won the lottery when they taste this, they should be killed. (Make sure you have ambrosia-makers on the jury and you'll get off scot-free.)

Of course (since he doesn't have to peel the oranges), Ludlow just loves ambrosia. So he has to put in his two-cents worth:

Now I know that making ambrosia is more trouble than having the preacher to dinner, but what would Christmas be without this delight? There hasn't been a Christmas in my life that I haven't had ambrosia.

When I was growing up, my Aunt Irene set the standard for good ambrosia.

If you'll make this at Christmas, you'll be more popular than St. Nick.

COMPNY'S COMIN'

Most cookbooks suggest trying Company Recipes on the family first. I don't know about you, but I'm not going to spend $100 or more and all day in the kitchen preparing Duck l'Orange for a bunch of brawling, sweaty kids who're bound to say, "Ewwww, I don't like that," as soon as they see it.

I prefer to experiment on grown-ups and take my chances. Normally that works out just fine, but one time it didn't.

There was a recipe in Joy of Cooking *called "Souffle or Puffed Potatoes" that sounded perfect to go with my Beef Wellington. It was a long, complicated recipe covering two pages, complete with diagrams showing exactly how to cut the potatoes. It even gave measurements for the slices, and required an electric deep fat fryer. (I borrowed one.) It called for "rendered kidney suet" (or vegetable oil, which I used because I'd never even* seen *kidney suet — and didn't care to, thank you.) I used a ruler to get the slices perfect. It was difficult and I threw a lot of potatoes-mistakes away. There must've been ten steps to the recipe, and I spent the better part of the day on it. When I was finally done, I had grease from one end of the kitchen to the other; second degree burns of varying sizes over my hands, arms, and left cheek; and what my mother would call "an attitude." The guests were seated in the dining room as the last of them came out of the fryer. If they'd been The Greatest Potatoes Ever Fried I would've been less irritable, but the fact of the matter was they were just plain potato chips.*

Probably the first and last time potato chips were served as an accompaniment to Beef Wellington.

 # Beef Wellington Dinner

Shrimp Remoulade Salad
Beef Wellington
Chateau Potatoes
Brussels Sprouts
Strawberry Pie
Cafe Juan More Cup

Beef Wellington is the first entrée in this chapter because it's my favorite to serve to special people.

When I decide on Beef Wellington, it means we're going to have to polish the silver and get down the good china, but it's worth it. When guests sit down at this table with the candles and flowers with the sparkling silver and crystal, they *know* they're very important people to me. A Beef Wellington is an important production and it looks like it and tastes like it.

But, it is easier than it looks.

Take the pastry for example: It's made the day before, it's easy to roll out, and if, like me, you're not good with pastries, this one can be rolled out a bit thicker so it won't tear. It's always beautiful.

The forcemeat is nothing but 15 things mixed together, and most of them are sitting in your cupboard right now. It can be made the day before the party, too.

The roast is expensive and I'm always afraid I'm going to ruin it. But somehow, I never have.

This recipe will serve a bunch of folks. I think six or eight people at the dinner table is perfect so I cut the tail-end of the roast off after it's cooked and save it for piroshki.

The Pastry

If you use the food processor no one will know.

4 cups flour
1 teaspoon salt
1/2 cup butter
1/2 cup shortening
1 egg, lightly beaten
ice water

Place the flour, salt, butter and shortening in a mixing bowl. Blend together with a pastry blender until the mixture looks like large bread crumbs. Add egg and enough ice water to make the mixture form a ball. Wrap in waxed paper and chill in the refrigerator. This should be made in advance and can be made the day before final preparation.

The Forcemeat Filling

¹/₄ cup butter or margarine
¹/₄ cup chopped onion
¹/₂ cup chopped mushrooms
¹/₄ cup cognac
¹/₂ pound finely ground veal
¹/₂ pound finely ground pork
1 egg, lightly beaten
¹/₄ cup heavy cream
¹/₄ cup chopped parsley
1 teaspoon salt
¹/₄ teaspoon basil
¹/₄ teaspoon thyme
¹/₄ teaspoon rosemary
¹/₈ teaspoon ground allspice
¹/₈ teaspoon pepper

Melt butter in a small saucepan. Add onion and cook till onion
is tender, but not brown. Stir in mushrooms and cognac. Cook
over medium heat 5-10 minutes. Turn mixture into a large
bowl. Add remaining ingredients and mix lightly but thoroughly. Cover and refrigerate until ready to use.

Beef Wellington

1 recipe pastry
1 whole beef tenderloin, 4-6 lbs
1 clove garlic, halved
salt and pepper
6 strips bacon

forcemeat filling
3-4 truffles, optional
1 egg lightly beaten

Heat oven to 450 degrees. Rub the filet all over with the cut side of the garlic. Sprinkle with salt and pepper. Cover with bacon strips and tie with string if necessary. Place on a rack in a roasting pan. Insert a meat thermometer in the thickest part of the meat. Roast 45-50 minutes or until the thermometer registers rare. Cool the meat slightly. Remove the bacon and put the meat in the refrigerator till later. Heat oven to 425 degrees. On a lightly floured board, roll the pastry into an 18 x 18-inch square, or large enough to enclose the beef. Lay the beef along one edge of the pastry. Cover with forcemeat. Cut truffles in halves and place along the top in a line. Lift the pastry up over the beef, overlapping it under the meat and sealing the edges. Trim off a few small ends of the pastry for garnish, if you want. Brush the edges with beaten egg to seal. Carefully place the beef on a baking sheet, sealed edge down. Cut the leftover pastry into decorations and arrange them on the pastry. Brush all over with the remaining beaten egg. Bake about 30 minutes, or until pastry is cooked and lightly browned. Remove carefully and cut into thick, crosswise slices and serve. Makes 10 to 12 servings.

 # Bearnaise Sauce

I should tell you that Knorr makes a Bearnaise Sauce mix that is every bit as good as this with less room for mistakes.

1/4 cup tarragon vinegar
1/4 cup dry white wine or dry Vermouth

2 teaspoons tarragon leaves
1 tablespoon chopped shallots
½ cup butter or margarine
1 egg
¼ teaspoon salt
pinch of cayenne

Combine vinegar, wine, tarragon leaves and shallots in a small stainless steel saucepan. Cook over low heat til mixture is reduced to two tablespoons. Remove from heat and cool, slightly. Melt the butter in the top of a double boiler over hot, not boiling water. Be sure that the bottom of the double boiler doesn't touch the water. Add egg, salt, cayenne and reduced liquid. Beat with a wire whisk until the mixture is smooth and thick. Remove from hot water and serve. Makes ¾ cup.

 # Shrimp Remoulade Salad

Arrange lettuce on a salad plate. Place four boiled, shelled and chilled shrimp on the plate; 5-6 cooked, chilled asparagus; and 3-4 thin slices of avocado. Put 3-4 tablespoons Remoulade sauce in the center:

1 cup mayonnaise
2 tablespoons Worcestershire sauce
3 teaspoons horseradish
3 tablespoons chopped parsley
garlic powder to taste
2 teaspoons red pepper
salt and pepper to taste

Just mix all the ingredients together and enjoy!

Chateau Potatoes

These are kind of "souped up" tater tots. I could eat them every meal. Diane never fixes enough of these to suit me. When I complain, she tells me to "Hush," that they are garnish.

They sure beat the heck out of parsley. (— Ludlow)

> potatoes
> 1 cup butter
> 1 cup vegetable oil
> salt to taste

Cut raw potatoes into balls with a melon scoop. Cook very slowly in a heavy skillet with lots of butter and oil until golden brown. Drain on paper towels and sprinkle with salt.

Don't try to cook enough of these for a full-fledged serving. They really should be a garnish.

 # Strawberry Custard Pie

This is a beautiful pie. Serve it with Cafe Juan More Cup.

> 1 package French vanilla pudding, instant
>   (3³/₄ ounces)
> 1 baked 10-inch pie shell, cooled
> 8 ladyfingers, split
> 1 pint strawberries
> 1 jar (10 ounces) red currant jelly
> whipped cream

Make the pudding as the directions say and pour it into the pie shell. Place the ladyfinger halves, cut side down, over the top of the pie filling. Hull the strawberries and cut in half. Arrange the berries, cut side down, on top of the ladyfingers close together. Heat the jelly with water until softened. Blend it till it is smooth and spoon it over the berries. Chill the pie till it's cold, several hours. Just before serving, border the pie with whipped cream.

 # Cafe Juan More Cup

This is the best coffee in the world. One cup of this and you'll want to punch Mrs. Folger right in the mouth and then go and set fire to the Maxwell House.

It's more trouble than plugging Mr. Coffee in, but it will absolutely knock your hat in the creek. It's that delicious.

Being a good Christian boy, I should tell you that you can't taste the 8 ounces of Cognac, but the fact of the matter is you can taste it, and it's delicious. (— Ludlow)

> *10 cups fresh brewed coffee*
> *3 sticks cinnamon*
> *1 peel of lemon . . . whole if you can do it*
> *1 whole orange*
> *cloves*
> *¼ cup sugar*
> *8 ounces cognac*

Stud the orange and lemon peel with cloves. Place into chafing dish with cinnamon and sugar. Heat the cognac. Pour into chafing dish and ignite. Stir until sugar melts and all ingredients are well blended. Slowly pour in hot coffee and continue to stir. Serve immediately.

Champignons Farcis Aux Crabes

24 *large white mushrooms*
4 *tablespoons freshly grated Parmesan cheese*
8 *ounces cream cheese*
4 *ounces Alaskan king crabmeat, drained, rinsed and*
   refreshed by tossing with 1 tablespoon lemon juice
2¹/₂ *tablespoons olive oil*
2 *tablespoons chopped fresh parsley*
1¹/₂ *tablespoons breadcrumbs*
juice of ¹/₂ lemon
1¹/₂ *teaspoon minced shallot*
1¹/₂ *teaspoon cognac*
1 *teaspoon Dijon mustard*
1 *teaspoon salt*
¹/₂ *teaspoon freshly ground pepper*
garlic butter, minced fresh parsley, and lemon wedges
   for garnish

Preheat the oven to 425 degrees. Lightly butter a large baking sheet. Remove mushroom stems. Combine 2 tablespoons Parmesan and the next 11 ingredients in a medium bowl and beat with electric mixer about 5 minutes. Fill the mushroom, forming a ¹/₂-inch dome on top of each. Arrange on a baking sheet and bake 10 minutes. Remove from oven and sprinkle with remaining 2 tablespoons Parmesan cheese. Preheat the broiler. Run the mushrooms under the broiler until Parmesan melts and is golden brown. Remove from oven and garnish.

Coquilles St. Jacques

Coquilles St. Jacques is one of my favorite dishes in the world. This is far and away the best I have ever had. Once you try this, you will be spoiled for any other recipe.

There are two things in the world that the French are expert in, and one of them is cooking. (—Ludlow)

> *1 cup dry white wine*
> *½ teaspoon salt*
> *grind of fresh pepper*
> *½ bay leaf*
> *2 tablespoons minced shallots or green onions*
> *1 pound sea scallops*
> *½ pound fresh mushrooms, sliced*
> *water*
> *butter*
> *4 tablespoons flour*
> *¾ cup milk*
> *2 egg yolks beaten*
> *½ cup heavy cream*
> *¼ cup grated Swiss cheese*

Combine wine, salt, pepper, bay leaf and shallots in an enameled saucepan. Bring to a boil and simmer 5 minutes. Add the scallops and mushrooms and enough water to just barely cover the scallops. Bring it to a boil, cover, lower the heat and simmer 5 minutes. Remove the scallops and mushrooms and set aside. Boil the remaining liquid down to about a cup. Remove the bay leaf. Melt 3 tablespoons butter in a saucepan. Stir in flour. Remove it from heat and slowly stir in the hot scallop liquid and the milk. Return to heat and cook, stirring constantly, until the mixture boils and is thickened and smooth. Beat together the egg yolks and cream. Beat some of the sauce into the egg yolks. Put all of that back into the mixture in the saucepan and cook over low heat, stirring constantly for 1 minute. Season with salt and pepper.

Cut the scallops into small pieces. Mix them into the sauce with mushrooms. Butter scallop shells or small individual casseroles. Fill them with the scallop mixture. Sprinkle cheese over the top of the shells. Dot each with a tablespoon of butter. Preheat the broiler. Put the broiler rack about 7 inches away from the heat source, and cook the shells until the sauce is bubbly and lightly browned. This serves between 4 and 6 people. Three or four if Ludlow is invited—maybe not that many.

 # Les Escargots Charles

I don't think I've ever had this dish. If I did, I didn't know what I was eating. I don't speak much French, but I think Les Escargots Charles translates out to "A Snail Named Chuck."

This may be okay, but on the face of it, it looks like a waste of brandy and French bread. (—Ludlow)

> *1 can escargots and shells, or fresh California snails*
> *red wine*
> *3 teaspoons minced onion*
> *1 stick butter*
> *1 tablespoon parsley*
> *1 clove garlic, crushed*
> *1 teaspoon Asbach Uralt or other brandy*

Clean and rinse snails and place in a saucepan. Cover with red wine, add onion, and cook on low heat for twenty minutes. In another pan, melt butter and add other ingredients. Place snails in shells or small dishes and pour butter sauce over them. Bake at 425 degrees until sauce is bubbling nicely. Serve with crusty French bread.

South African Rock Lobster Thermidor

Besides tasting great (the best Lobster Thermidor I've ever had) this is a favorite because all of the work can be done before the guests arrive. I'd much rather laugh and talk in the living room than be slogging away in the kitchen.

> *2 packages rock lobster tails (9 ounces each)*
> *boiling water*
> *1 tablespoon whole pickling spice*
> *1/4 cup butter or margarine*
> *1/3 cup flour*
> *1 can (10 1/2 ounces) condensed chicken broth*
> *3/4 cup heavy cream*
> *2 tablespoons sherry*
> *1 tablespoon brandy*
> *8 ounces fresh sauteed mushrooms*
> *salt and pepper*
> *1/4 cup grated fresh Parmesan cheese*

Drop the lobster tails into a large pot of boiling water that already has the pickling spice in it. When the water comes back to a boil, take out the lobster and dunk it into cold water. When the lobster tails are cool, cut away the underside membrane of each tail, and remove the meat. Dice the lobster meat. Melt the butter in a saucepan and stir in the flour and cook for 1 minute. Remove it from the heat. Gradually stir in the chicken broth and cream. Add the sherry and brandy. Cook it over low heat, stirring constantly, until the sauce thickens and comes to a boil. Remove it from heat, and gently stir in the mushrooms and lobster meat. Season with salt and pepper to taste. Reheat it thoroughly, then spoon it back into the lobster shells. Sprinkle with Parmesan cheese. Preheat the broiler and broil the tails until golden brown. It's wonderful! Serves 8.

Swedish Meatballs with Burgundy Wine

I stand with Will Rogers, who once said, "I never met a meatball I didn't like."

I am an absolute hog about meatballs and have never tasted better than these.

This recipe makes about 30 delicious meatballs, just enough for a light, little snack. (— Ludlow)

1 pound ground chuck or round steak
1 cup dried bread crumbs
1 egg, beaten (very large)
1 cup light cream
1 small onion, chopped very fine
1 teaspoon cornstarch
1¼ teaspoons salt
4 tablespoons salad oil
3 tablespoons flour
2 cups water
1 cup Burgundy
2 beef bouillon cubes or 3 cubes if needed for taste
2 teaspoons sugar
pepper to taste

Combine meat, onion crumbs, cornstarch, egg, cream, half the salt and pepper and shape into 30 to 34 balls. Drop balls, a few at a time, into hot fat in skillet. Brown well on all sides, then transfer to a hot plate. Stir the flour into remainder of fat in the skillet, then add the bouillon cubes, water, sugar, burgundy, salt. Cook on very low heat, stirring until smooth. Arrange meatballs in the sauce, cover, and simmer for 30 minutes. These can be made the day before serving and then reheated.

Oysters Rockefeller

If you must eat oysters, this is a good way to do it. Even if you're not big on oysters, by the time you add Tabasco to taste, you can put a little kick in these bad boys.

Serving this dish to company makes them feel special, unless you get too much Tabasco; then it can make them drink more of the cheap wine you've been trying to get rid of since 1947. (— Ludlow)

> *36 oysters*
> *1 pound or 2 10-ounce packages fresh spinach*
> *1 cup finely chopped scallions*
> *½ cup finely chopped celery*
> *½ cup finely chopped parsley*
> *1 clove garlic, finely minced*
> *1 2-ounce can anchovies, drained*
> *8 tablespoons butter*
> *1 tablespoon flour*
> *½ cup heavy cream*
> *Tabasco sauce*
> *1-2 tablespoons Pernod or Ricard or some kind of*
>   *anise flavored liqueur*
> *⅓ cup grated FRESH Parmesan cheese*

Preheat oven to 450 degrees. Open the oysters, making sure they stay on the half-shell, and save the oyster liquor. Take the spinach and pick out any tough stems or bad leaves. Rinse the leaves and put in a saucepan. Cover and cook till they are wilted. Drain them well, and squeeze them to get rid of all the moisure. (They have got to be slap dry.) Blend them or chop them up so that there is about 2 cups. Put the scallions, celery and parsley into the container of an electric blender and chop them up. There should be about a cup. Chop the garlic and anchovies together.

Heat 4 tablespoons of butter in a frying pan and add the scallion and celery mixture. After about a minute, add the anchovy mixture. After another minute, add the spinach. Stir it up. In another pan, heat the other 4 tablespoons of butter and add the flour. Stir it with a wire whisk and add the oyster liquor. Stir in the cream. Put in as much Tabasco as you like. Make sure you don't add salt. Stir in the spinach mixture and Pernod. Let the whole thing cool. Spoon the same amount of the mixture on to the top of the oysters and sprinkle with Parmesan cheese. Bake for about 25 minutes or until piping hot. They are delicious!

The first time we tried this Ludlow shucked the oysters for me. He got plenty of little cuts but only one really bad one; nonetheless, his immortal soul is surely in danger from the language he used. Since then I've bought the shucked, raw oysters at a seafood restaurant near us. They don't mind doing all the work and Lud's celestial future is in less jeopardy.

 # Crown Pork Roast

The first step is the hardest: find the finest meat cutter in town and take him some homemade cookies. Your butcher is the key factor with this roast. He's got to form it perfectly, cut off the unnecessary fat, and "French" the bones on the top (i.e., cut off the meat around the bones that make the crown).

When you bring the roast home, cook it according to the tables in your big, fat cookbook. Use a meat thermometer. Cover the tips of the crown individually with wadded up aluminum foil so they won't burn. I bake it unstuffed, on a rack, bones up.

When it's done, I stuff it with dried mixed fruit that I've cooked and then mashed. I garnish it with fresh fruits.

Those wonderful kitchen stores in the malls sell the little white paper things to put on the bones that look like crowns. Or, you can make your own with aluminum foil, as follows: Fold a six-inch strip of heavy foil lengthwise and cut in half. On the fold, cut into the foil about 2½ inches every ½ inch or so. Roll the uncut end around two fingers and then pull the folds apart to form crown-like points. Make one for each bone, or make them for half the bones and cover every other one with canned kumquats.

This roast is so pretty that guests are likely to gasp!

 # Ludlow's Prime Rib on the Grill

If you really want to show off for company fix a prime rib on your grill. It's easy and your guests will think you're a master chef.

It's going to take two hours to cook it properly, maybe more, so allow enough time.

After you get your coals going, put a piece of heavy duty aluminum foil (folded up on the sides so the grease won't run out), that's about the same size as the roast on the grill. Put the roast, bone side down on the foil. Put the lid on it and go away for awhile. Don't turn the roast. About the only thing you may have to do is spoon some of the grease off the paper.

After an hour and a half or so, stick a meat thermometer in and check it. 130 is rare, 140 is medium, 150 is done.

It's just that simple and you'll get good results every time.

Vichyssoise

If you don't try any other recipe in this book, you ought to try this "cold tater soup" — as they call it in Alabama. Let me warn you in advance, no matter how much of this you make, it ain't going to be enough. It's so good it'll make your shirttail run up your back like a window shade.

We always make a lot more than we're going to have for supper and eat along on it for days. (It's a perfect snack while you're watching football on TV.)

Don't serve this too often because it's loaded with calories and will make your waist large — but it's worth it.
(— Ludlow)

>*3 leeks*
>*2 tablespoons margarine*
>*1 small onion sliced*
>*1/2 cup chicken stock*
>*1/2 cup water*
>*2 teaspoons salt*
>*4 medium potatoes, peeled and sliced*
>*1 1/2 cups milk*
>*1 1/2 cups Half & Half*
>*3/4 cup whipping cream*
>*chopped chives for garnish*

Wash the leeks and remove the roots and the green part. Slice thin. Melt the margarine in a large pot and saute the onion in it. (Add more margarine if you need to.) Add chicken broth, water, salt and potatoes. Bring to a boil and simmer for 40 minutes, until the potatoes are tender. Pour into a blender and process until smooth. Return to the pot. Add milk and Half & Half. Bring just to the boiling point but DO NOT BOIL.

Cool mixture. Run through a fine strainer. When the soup is cold add the whipping cream. I make this the day before so it will be icy at serving time.

 # Baked Alaska

My Baked Alaska is the best I've ever had. The recipe is a closely guarded secret. People far and wide have come to slobber over it.

I cannot possibly reveal the secret, but I'll give you a small hint: Baskin Robbins.

BREADS

I have had a weight problem for the better part of my life. The main reason for it is bread. It is not enough to say I love bread. If I don't have bread, I feel like I haven't eaten. If I had been born 5000 years ago, I would have started a religion that worshipped loaf bread.

I think you will like all the bread recipes in this chapter with the possible exception of the Zucchini bread. I don't know a whole lot about squash, but I do know that you're not supposed to make bread out of it.

The recipe for Mexican cornbread is wonderful. I would give you one word of warning. The recipe calls for 3 jalapeno peppers, seeded and chopped. If you miss one or two seeds, it could very well change your life.

But first comes Diane's world-class loaf bread, and I can promise you two things about this recipe. One: it is delicious; it may just be the best bread you ever put in the middle of your mouth. Two: when you set out to make this bread, you had better be in good physical condition, cause when you start to push, pull, and turn, you are going to be doing something that's about one step above "stoop labor." If you are into good bread and tough conditioning, this recipe is for you.

 Diane's Loaf Bread

I was an eighteen-year-old half-wit when I made my first loaf of bread, from *this* recipe, I might add. It was beautiful and delicious. Follow the directions to the letter. Use bread flour. Trust me, it'll be wonderful!

Rinse a large mixing bowl with hot water to get it warm. Put in it ½ cup lukewarm water (110 degrees) and 1 package yeast. Let it stand for 5 minutes then stir it. In another bowl, mix:

1 cup milk
1 cup boiling water
2 tablespoons butter or margarine
2 tablespoons sugar
1 tablespoon salt

Stir until lukewarm. Add this to the yeast mixture and stir. Add three cups of bread flour and mix thoroughly.

Add three more cups of bread flour, slowly, constantly mixing it as you go. It should pull away from the sides of the bowl to form a ball. If it doesn't, add more bread flour a tablespoon at a time until it does. Put ½ cup of bread flour on your mixing board or counter top. Dust very lightly and push the rest of the flour to the side for later use. Dump the dough out of the bowl onto the board and cover the dough with the inverted bowl. You and the dough need a ten-minute rest.

You can knead bread, and you know how. The information may be locked in your genes, but it's there. Mankind has been doing it since the time of the ancient Egyptians, right up until the last few generations. You'll catch on right away.

Go back to the dough and lift the bowl. It will look more "relaxed" than it did when you covered it. Wash the bowl and dry it. Grease it heavily with butter or margarine and set it aside. Grease your hands and wrists. Use your fingertips to fold the dough toward yourself, then use the heel of your hands to push it down and away from you. Again, pull and fold the dough toward yourself turning it slightly. Push, pull and turn. Push, pull and turn. The rhythm is soothing, like rocking a baby, except more vigorous. Get your back into it. Put more flour on the board as the dough begins to stick and put more butter on your hands.

After 7 or 8 minutes, stop. Notice how the dough looks and feels. Next time you won't have to watch the clock. Pick the dough up in your greased hand, hold your hand out flat. If you can hold it for 30 seconds without having it stick, you're through kneading.

Your greased bowl should be large enough to hold three times the amount of dough you have. Plop the dough in it and mash it down. Turn the dough over so that the top will be lightly greased. Cover the bowl with a damp dishcloth.

It needs to rise in a warm place (80-85 degrees). Since no such place exists in my home, I put it on a rack in the oven with a bowl of hot water on the floor of the oven. It will double in size in 1½ hours.

When the dough has risen, take the towel off. Grease your finger and poke the dough. If the dent stays in the bread it is ready to work with. Flour your board, grease your hands and gird your loins; it's time to get tough.

Make a fist and punch the dough down into the bowl. Fold the edges in and dump it out onto your floured board. Slap it hard several times. (All this punching and slapping is to release the gasses from the bread and the hostilities in you. I'm convinced that breadmaking kept our ancestors saner than we are).

Divide the dough into 2 pieces. Grease two loaf pans. Mash 1 piece into each pan. Turn it greased side up again. Cover with your damp dishcloth. Let it rise again. (The temperature should be 75-80 degrees. Any warmer and your bread will have a heavy seam in the bottom.) This time it will take about an hour for it to double its size.

To bake, preheat the oven to 400 degrees (350 degrees if you're using glass pans). Bake for 40-60 minutes. When it is done, it will sound hollow if you tap the bottom of the pans. Brush butter on the tops of the loaves and put them back in the oven for 2-3 minutes. Bring them out and lay the loaves on their sides on a rack to cool. When you can't stand it another minute, get out the butter and eat a loaf!

 # Buttermilk Biscuits

Biscuits should be made with lard. Lard will kill you. Some things are worth dying for.

2 cups sifted flour
2 teaspoons baking powder
¹/₄ teaspoon soda

³/₄ teaspoon salt
¹/₄ cup lard
about 1 cup buttermilk

Heat the oven to 475 degrees. Sift together the flour, baking powder, salt and soda. Cut in lard until mixture looks like coarse corn meal. Stir in buttermilk with a fork until a soft dough forms. Knead and roll out onto a lightly floured board. Cut to desired thickness. Bake about 10 minutes.

Cheese-Onion Supper Bread

This is great to have with dried beans instead of corn-bread. As a matter of fact, this is great to have with anything.

¹/₂ cup chopped onion
1 beaten egg
¹/₂ cup milk
1¹/₂ cup biscuit mix
1 cup shredded sharp cheese
2 tablespoons snipped parsley
2 tablespoons melted butter

Saute onion in oil until tender, but not brown. Combine egg and milk and add that to biscuit mix. Stir only until moist. Add onion and half of the cheese and parsley. Spread the dough into an 8-inch greased round pan. Sprinkle cheese on top. Dribble butter over the whole thing. Bake at 400 degrees for 20 minutes or until a toothpick comes out clean.

Diane's Cornbread

When writing a book, one is moved to leave one's mark upon the world. One wishes to enlighten and pontificate about the profound. This is my chance and I must take it—damn the consequences. My words of wisdom for the world are:

Cake's sweet, cornbread ain't.

If you put sugar in your cornbread, people are going to talk about you behind your back. It's as simple as that. Here is a recipe for *real* cornbread:

> *1 egg, beaten lightly*
> *2 cups of cornmeal mix (if you're a purist, buy plain cornmeal and add your own baking powder and salt)*
> *1¹/₂ cups milk*
> *2 tablespoons bacon grease (no substitions)*

Add all the wet ingredients to the cornmeal. Stir well. Preheat the oven to 400 degrees. Put another 2 tablespoons of bacon grease in your iron skillet, put it in the oven to heat the skillet and melt the grease. Take it out, roll the grease around the pan with a few crumpled paper towels. Pour the cornbread batter in and bake until it's nice and brown, 20-25 minutes.

Ludlow's Cornbread and Buttermilk

This is another easy-to-fix slice of Heaven. The first thing you do is fix a wagon load of Diane's cornbread. Next, put a big slice of cornbread into a large glass, pour fresh cold buttermilk over the bread and salt and pepper to taste. Eat it with a spoon. Spring onions on the side make this even more appealing.

WARNING: Always wash the glass immediately after you finish. If you leave an empty buttermilk glass around, your wife and children will make fun of you and exclude you from all family activities.

 # Fried Cornbread

Mix cornmeal mix, onion, an egg, milk (or even water). Put enough liquid in it to make it like pancake batter. Melt some bacon grease in your big iron skillet and fry it the same way you would a pancake.

This is good when you don't have enough people to eat a whole pan of cornbread, or when you want something different.

French Bread

¹/₄ cup warm water
1 package dry yeast
1 teaspoon salt
2 teaspoons sugar
1 tablespoon shortening dissolved in 1 cup hot water
3¹/₄ cups sifted flour

Dissolve the yeast in the water. Add one cup of flour to liquified shortening mixture and beat well. Add the yeast liquid and beat well. Fold in one egg white, beaten. Add remaining flour and beat until stiff. Let the dough rest on a floured board for 5 minutes. Knead 7 to 10 minutes and add flour if needed to make the dough firm. Place in a greased bowl and turn once. Let the dough rise 1 hour. Punch down, cut dough in half and roll into equal strips; twist together 3 times. Put into a greased baking dish and let rise 1 hour or until doubled in bulk. Bake for 40 minutes at 375 degrees.

 # Sour Cream Biscuits

If you believe you can't make a decent homemade biscuit, try these. They melt in your mouth.

2 cups Bisquick
8 ounces sour cream
¹/₄ pound butter, melted
1 egg

Mix all ingredients by hand. Drop by tablespoons onto greased cookie sheet. Baket at 450 degrees for about 12 minutes or until golden brown.

 # Mexican Cornbread

1 cup self-rising cornmeal
¹/₂ teaspoon soda
¹/₂ teaspoon salt
¹/₂ teaspoon sugar
3 eggs, beaten
1 cup milk
3 jalapeno peppers, seeded and chopped
¹/₂ cup chopped onion
1¹/₂ cup shredded Cheddar cheese
1 teaspoon garlic powder
1 7-ounce can whole kernel corn, drained
1 2-ounce jar chopped pimento, drained
¹/₃ cup bacon drippings

Combine cornmeal, soda, salt and sugar; stir in remaining ingredients. Pour into a greased 10-inch iron skillet. Bake at 350 degrees for 45 minutes or until golden brown. Makes 12 to 15 servings.

Refrigerator Rolls

So called because the dough will last in the refrigerator for a couple of weeks. Very handy.

> *⅔ cup butter*
> *1 cup milk, scalded*
> *½ cup sugar*
> *1 teaspoon salt*
> *2 eggs, well beaten*
> *1 cup mashed potatoes*
> *1 package yeast, dissolved in ¼ cup warm water*
> *4 cups plain flour*

Melt the butter and add to scalded milk. Add sugar and salt. Let cool to lukewarm. Add remaining ingredients. Almost enough flour has been added when the dough is hard to stir. Put the dough on a floured surface. Add flour until dough will not stick to the surface. Knead until smooth and elastic. Put dough in a bowl to rise until double in size, or you may put the dough in the refrigerator to use later. After dough has doubled, roll out and shape rolls. Place on baking sheet, and let rise again. Bake at 400 degrees for 20 minutes, or until browned.

Zucchini Bread

3 eggs
1 cup sugar
1 cup dark brown sugar
1 cup vegetable oil
1 tablespoon vanilla
2 cups zucchini, unpeeled, grated, and drained
1¹/₂ cup all-purpose flour
¹/₂ cup whole wheat flour
¹/₄ teaspoon baking powder
2 teaspoons baking soda
1 teaspoon salt
1 tablespoon cinnamon
¹/₂ cup chopped cashews
¹/₄ cup wheat germ

Beat eggs until fluffy and add both types of sugar, oil, and vanilla. Blend well. Stir in zucchini. Sift together the flour, wheat flour, baking powder, baking soda, salt, and cinnamon. Blend into liquid mixture. Add nuts and wheat germ and blend until combined. Bake in two greased and floured small loaf pans at 350 degrees for 1-1¹/₂ hours or until knife inserted into the center comes out cleanly.

HOT DANG! IT'S PARTY TIME

If you are not good at parties, read this chapter carefully and you will come off like the "hostess with the mostest." There's enough delicious party food in these pages to have fed all the White House guests during the Reagan years.

Of course, the most important ingredient to a good party is the people you invite. The good party starts with a good guest list, and as a matter of fact, if the guest list is good enough, you can serve raw weenies and Nu-Grape. If you're not sure about the list, then you better serve everything in this chapter.

The perfect guest list is one that mixes people who don't know each other. This gives them something to talk about. You'd be amazed how well your doctor and your mechanic hit it off.

The only big mistake I ever made was inviting a liberal to a party. When my cousin Doodle found out the guy had not voted for Barry Goldwater, he went after him with one of those little hors d'oeuvre swords. Yes sir, the guest list is very important.

 ## Appetizer Puffs

¹/₄ cup butter or margarine
¹/₂ cup water
¹/₂ cup all purpose flour
¹/₈ teaspoon salt
2 eggs

Lightly grease 2 large baking sheets and set aside. Preheat the oven to 400 degrees. In a medium saucepan, heat the butter and water to a rolling boil. Add flour and salt all at once. Stir vigorously over low heat about 1 minute or until the mixture becomes smooth and leaves the sides of the pan. Remove from heat. Beat in the eggs, one at a time. Beat the mixture until it loses its gloss. On the prepared cookie sheet, drop the dough by mounded teaspoonfuls making four rows with four mounds in each row. Bake about 15 minutes until puffed and lightly browned.

For a tasty deviled ham filling, just blend together 1 package (3 ounces) of cream cheese, 1 can deviled ham, 1 tablespoon chili sauce, and ¹/₂ teaspoon prepared mustard.

Artichoke With Shrimp

mayonnaise
curry powder
artichoke
lemon
garlic
salt
cooked shrimp (the teeny, tiny ones)

Mix mayonnaise and curry to taste. Boil the artichoke for 45 minutes with lemon, garlic and salt. Put a dot of the mayonnaise mixture on the stalk end of each leaf. Top with one tiny shrimp.

Bacon-Wrapped Water Chestnuts

2 10-ounce cans of water chestnuts
1 5-ounce bottle soy sauce
granulated sugar
1 pound bacon

Marinate water chestnuts in soy sauce for at least 3 hours, turning often. Roll in sugar. Wrap each water chestnut in ½ strip bacon (don't stretch the bacon). Secure the bacon with toothpicks. Bake at 400 degrees for 15-20 minutes, or until bacon is partially crisp. Serve hot. These can be made ahead and refrigerated until time to bake and serve. Also note that chicken livers can be substituted for water chestnuts. Makes 35-40.

California Gouda

Pat Jones cut this out of Jean Thwaite's column in the paper, made the dish and brought it to our Christmas party. It's wonderful!

> *1 round Gouda cheese*
> *1 4-roll package refrigerated crescent rolls*
> *1 jar hot pepper jelly*
> *Triscuits*

Remove red wax from the Gouda. Unwrap the crescent rolls and pinch together the seams to form two rectangles. Wrap the rolls around the cheese in two sheets until cheese is encrusted. Bake for 10-12 minutes at 375 degrees until crust is golden. Remove from oven and serve with pepper jelly on top. Serve hot on Triscuit crackers.

 # Beverly's Cheese Chex

Melt 5 tablespoons butter in a big pot. Add a good sprinkle of salt and then 6 cups of Corn Chex and stir like crazy. Add ⅓ cup fresh grated Parmesan cheese. Stir over heat until cheese is melted. Pour out on foil and separate to cool. If you can stand over it and not eat it, you're a better person than I.

Beverly (Morgan) says you can use any kind of Chex flavors, but this one is so good, it's the only one I've tried.

Aunt Barbara's Cheese Rounds

¹/₂ pound grated sharp Cheddar cheese
1 stick oleo
3 tablespoons dry onion soup mix
1 cup regular flour

Mix all ingredients together and shape into a roll. Chill thoroughly. Slice into thin slices and place on a cookie sheet. Bake in a 375 degree oven for 10-15 minutes. Makes about 4 dozen and they also freeze well.

Chili Con Quesa

1 pound Velveeta
1 pound hot pepper cheese
1 can Ro-tel tomatoes
salt
1-2 teaspoons Jalapeno relish

Melt the cheeses, add tomatoes, salt to taste, and jalapeno pepper relish. Serve in a chafing dish with plain Doritos.

Crab Stuffed Mushrooms

1 pound large mushrooms (about 20)
¹/₂ cup bottled Italian dressing
1 tablespoon butter
1 7¹/₂-ounce can crabmeat, drained and flaked
³/₄ cup coarse, fresh bread crumbs
2 eggs slightly beaten
¹/₄ cup minced onion
¹/₄ cup mayonnaise
1 teaspoon lemon juice
¹/₂ teaspoon salt

Marinate the mushroom caps in dressing for an hour. Mince the stems and saute in butter. Drain the mushroom caps. Mix crabmeat, ¹/₂ cup bread crumbs, eggs, onion, mayonnaise, lemon juice, salt and mushroom stems. Place the mushroom caps in a shallow baking dish. Fill the caps with the crab mixture. Top with remaining bread crumbs. Bake at 375 degrees for 15 minutes.

 # Diane's Dilled Shrimp

This is *my* favorite recipe, and I can promise that none will be left over. I also believe that any recipe that can be made the night before the party is a blessing.

1¹/₂ cups mayonnaise
¹/₃ cup lemon juice
¹/₄ cup sugar
¹/₂ cup dairy sour cream
1 large red onion, sliced thinly
2 tablespoons dry dill
¹/₄ teaspoon salt
3 pounds cooked medium shrimp

In a big bowl, mix the mayonnaise, lemon juice, sugar, sour cream, onion, dill and salt. Stir in the shrimp. Cover it and refrigerate overnight. Stir it once and serve.

Heidi's Dip

Another Pat Jones specialty. She made this for Charlie's graduation celebration and it was gone before anyone even looked at the rest of the buffet.

2 cups chopped onions
2 cups grated Swiss cheese (you can use Cheddar)
2 cups Hellman's mayo (must be Hellman's)

Mix well and bake 350 degrees for about 30 minutes. Serve with French bread torn into bite size.

Marilyn's Super Ham Dip

Marilyn Proehl brought this to our New Year's Eve Party. I considered hiding it in the refrigerator so I could have all of it.

1 8-ounce package cream cheese
1 can (6³/₄ ounces) Hormel chunk ham
2 teaspoons fresh Vidalia onion
2 teaspoons fresh parsley
4 teaspoons milk
1 teaspoon powdered horseradish
dash of garlic powder
dash of celery salt
dash of black pepper

Have the cheese at room temperature. Add remaining ingredients and mix until thoroughly blended. Serve with toasted bread rounds or crackers.

 # Ham Puffs

1 (8-ounce) package cream cheese
1 egg yolk, beaten
1 teaspoon onion juice
¹/₂ teaspoon baking powder
salt to taste
¹/₄ teaspoon horseradish
¹/₄ teaspoon hot sauce
24 small bread rounds
2 (2¹/₄-ounce) cans deviled ham

Blend together the first seven ingredients. Toast the bread rounds on one side. Spread the untoasted side with deviled ham and cover each with a mound of the cheese mixture. Place on a cookie sheet, and bake at 375 degrees for 10-12 minutes or until puffed and brown. Serve hot.

 # Sweet & Sour Meatballs

1 pound lean ground beef
1 chopped onion
1 egg
salt and pepper
10 ounces chili sauce
10 ounces grape jelly
1 lemon

Mix the first 4 ingredients together and form into balls. Mix the last three ingredients and cook the meatballs in this sauce. Serve in a chafing dish.

(I usually make a second batch of the sauce to serve the meatballs in because the sauce it's cooked in loses its color and zip.)

Onion Delight

2 Vidalia onions
¹/₂ cup sugar
1 cup apple cider vinegar
2 cups water
¹/₂ cup mayonnaise
¹/₂ teaspoon dill seed
1 package (3 ounces) cream cheese
¹/₂ box Ritz crackers

Chop the onions and mix in sugar, vinegar and water. Marinate overnight, or at least 4 hours. Before serving, drain well, then mix in mayonnaise and dill seed. Spread crackers with cream cheese and then spread the onion mixture. Makes 24 cocktail appetizers.

 # Judy Merritt's Party Treats

1 stick oleo
1 cup chocolate chips
1 cup smooth peanut butter
1 large box Crispix cereal
1 box powdered sugar

Melt the first three ingredients until smooth. Pour over the cereal. Pour out onto waxed paper and separate to cool. Put coated cereal with sugar in a bag and shake.

Piroshki

This recipe makes the *best* Piroshki we've ever had … including the ones at restaurants that specialize in them. They're always a hit at a cocktail party, but you can make six large ones and have it as an entrée.

> 1 10-ounce package frozen patty shells
> 2 tablespoons butter or margarine
> 1/4 cup coarse chopped onion
> 3 tablespoons sour cream
> 1¼ cups coarsely shredded cooked roast beef
> 1/2 teaspoon dried dillweed
> 1/2 teaspoon salt, dash pepper
> 1 egg yolk

Remove patty shells from package; let stand at room temperature 30 minutes to soften. Meanwhile, in hot butter in a small skillet, saute onion 2 minutes. Add onions and butter to 3 tablespoons sour cream, the shredded beef, dill, salt and pepper. Mix well; reserve. Preheat oven to 425 degrees. On a lightly floured pastry cloth, roll each patty shell to make oblong 8 by 5 inches; cut in half crosswise. Spread a rounded tablespoon meat filling on half of each piece. Fold over filling; crimp to seal edges and cut tiny slits in top. Place on cookie sheet lined with heavy brown paper. Brush with egg yolk beaten with 1 tablespoon water. Bake 15 minutes, or until golden. Serve with Bearnaise sauce on the side. Makes 12.

Sausage Balls

This old tried-and-true recipe is Lud's favorite. One year at our Christmas open house I set them on the coffee table seconds after taking them out of the oven—I mean the grease was still sizzling on them. I said, "Let them cool a few minutes," but Hugh Baby Jarrett didn't hear me. Not only does Hugh Baby remember, everybody there remembers. Poor Hugh.

> *1 12-ounce package hot bulk sausage*
> *1 pound Cheddar cheese, shredded*
> *1 cup buttermilk biscuit mix*

Preheat the oven to 350 degrees. In a mixing bowl, mix up the sausage, cheese and biscuit mix. Don't use a food processor, it doesn't come out right. Shape the dough into walnut-sized balls and bake 35 to 45 minutes until lightly browned. You can serve these immediately, or you can freeze them for later.

 # Spinach Dip

> *1 pint dairy sour cream*
> *1 cup mayonnaise*
> *³/₄ package dry leek soup mix, about ¹/₂ cup*
> *1 10-ounce package frozen chopped spinach, drained well*
> *¹/₂ cup chopped parsley*
> *¹/₂ cup chopped green onions*

1 teaspoon dry dill
1 teaspoon dry Italian salad dressing mix
your favorite vegetables cut up, raw

In a big bowl, or in a food processor, combine all the ingredients except the raw vegetables, until blended well. Refrigerate the dip until you're ready to serve it. It will keep for about two days. Serve the dip with the raw vegetables. It makes about 3½ cups.

 # Spinach Balls

2 packages frozen chopped spinach, cooked and
    drained well.
2 cups Pepperidge Farm seasoned dressing
4 eggs, beaten
1 large onion, chopped
¼ cup melted butter or margarine
½ cup Parmesan cheese
½ teaspoon Accent
¼ teaspoon thyme
½ teaspoon pepper
½ teaspoon garlic salt

Mix together and chill overnight. Roll into balls. Bake 30 minutes at 350 degrees, 40 minutes if the balls are frozen. Makes about 50 balls.

Tostado Dip

2 cans bean dip
2 or 3 avocados
2 tablespoons lemon juice
1 8-ounce container of sour cream
minced scallions
8 ounces taco sauce (mild)
2 tomatoes chopped
1 pound shredded Cheddar cheese

Mash the avocado and mix with lemon juice. Layer all the ingredients in the order listed. Serve with tostado chips. (You can also add chopped black olives.)

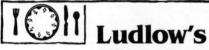

Ludlow's Plugged Watermelon

After the 4th of July, buy a big, green watermelon. (If it's ripe, it'll sound hollow when you thump it.) Cut a hole in the watermelon, pour rum in the hole until it won't hold anymore. Replace the hole cover. Put it in the refrigerator for at least eight hours.

If you don't like rum, you probably won't like plugged watermelon. Of course, if you don't like watermelon, you won't like it either.

WARNING: Do not drop!

Carl's Ultimate Egg Nog

12 eggs separated
1 quart whipping cream
1 quart whiskey
1 quart coffee cream
¼ cup rum
1 cup sugar

To the yolks, add all of the sugar at one time. Beat and beat the mixture until it's light colored, thick and smooth. When the eggs and sugar have been beaten together to the right consistency, add whiskey a little at a time, beating vigorously. Add all the rum and beat again. Add coffee cream. Whip the whipping cream and fold into the mixture. Beat the egg whites until stiff. Fold them into the mixture. Let it stand to ripen. This can be made two days ahead of time.

FOR THE SWEET TOOTH

I do have a real sweet tooth, but generally speaking, when I eat about 2 or 3 mouthfuls of something sweet, it will take care of it.

However, when I find a really good dessert, it usually takes a 40 gallon vat to fill me up.

When I was growing up, rice pudding and banana pudding were two of the big desserts served at our house. My Mama Kidd was famous far and wide for her blackberry cobbler. The crust on her cobbler was sent straight from Heaven. When my Uncle Chuck made homemade ice cream, I was the first one to show up and turn the freezer handle. I didn't do it because I was a workaholic; I did it because I wanted to be the one who got to lick the dasher.

I have a theory. I don't think the Japanese work any harder than we do. I think if they get to work early and stay late, their boss lets them lick the dasher.

Micro-Baked Apple

2 large baking apples
2 teaspoons butter or margarine
4 teaspoons brown sugar
1/2 teaspoon cinnamon
2 teaspoons golden raisins
2 tablespoons water

Core apples and make a slit in the skin all around the middle of each apple to prevent the skin from bursting. Place apples in a small baking dish. In a small bowl, melt butter on High for 10 seconds. Stir in sugar, cinnamon and raisins. Fill each apple with sugar mixture. Add water to the dish and cook, covered with plastic wrap, on High 4 to 5 minutes.

 # Blackberry Wine Cake

1 Duncan Hines white cake mix
1 box blackberry Jello
1/2 cup blackberry wine
4 eggs
1 cup oil
1 cup pecans, chopped

Grease and flour a tube pan. Place nuts in the bottom of the pan. Mix all other ingredients and pour the mixture over the nuts. Bake at 325 degrees for 50 minutes or till done. Glaze as follows:

¹/₂ cup blackberry wine
¹/₂ box granulated sugar
¹/₂ stick margarine

Bring all ingredients to a boil. As soon as you take the cake out of the oven, pour half the glaze over the cake. Wait 30 minutes, then turn cake out of the pan and pour the other half of the glaze on that side. The cake tastes better after a day or two, and it freezes well.

 # Blueberry Cake

¹/₂ cup butter
3 eggs
1 tablespoon baking powder
1 teaspoon nutmeg
¹/₂ cup blueberries
¹/₂ cup honey
2³/₄ cups whole wheat pastry flour
2 teaspoons cinnamon
¹/₂ cup walnuts
1¹/₄ cups 2% milk

Cream together butter and honey. Add milk and eggs and mix until smooth. Sift together flour, baking powder, cinnamon and nutmeg. Add to creamed mixture. Add blueberries and walnuts and mix until all ingredients are just moistened. Pour into lightly oiled and floured cake pans and bake at 350 degrees for 25-30 minutes.

For blueberry ricotta frosting:

2 cups ricotta cheese
¹/₄ cup honey plus 4 packages Equal sweetener
1 tablespoon arrowroot
3 tablespoons water
2 cups blueberries
1 teaspoon vanilla

In a small pan, dissolve arrowroot in water. Cook in double boiler till thickened. Mix together ricotta, blueberries, honey and vanilla. Add cooled arrowroot mixture to the rest and blend thoroughly in a food processor. Cover and refrigerate for at least 2 hours. Frost blueberry cake.

Bread Pudding With Custard Sauce

4 slices buttered bread
2 eggs beaten
¹/₃ cup sugar
¹/₄ teaspoon salt
3 cups milk
¹/₃ cup raisins

Mix the eggs, sugar, salt and raisins and pour the mixture over the bread. Let it stand for 30 minutes. Bake at 325 degrees for 30 minutes covered, then 30 minutes uncovered.

This custard sauce is special over pound cake, bread pudding, rice pudding or anything else. It's good hot or cold. The one who stirs while it's thickening gets to lick the pot.

Combine 3 beaten egg yolks, ¼ cup sugar and a dash of salt. Stir in 2 cups scalded milk. Cook in a double boiler, stirring constantly until the mixture coats a spoon. Add 1 teaspoon vanilla.

 # Gooey Butter Cake

1 (17-ounce) box pound cake mix
½ cup butter, melted
4 eggs
1 (8-ounce) package cream cheese
½ teaspoon vanilla extract
1 pound confectioners' sugar
1 cup chopped nuts

Combine the cake mix, butter and 2 eggs, stirring well until blended. Beat 1 minute. Spread batter in a greased 13 x 9 inch baking pan. Beat cream cheese with electric mixer until light and fluffy. Beat in remaining 2 eggs, then vanilla. Set aside ½ cup confectioners' sugar. Beat remaining sugar into cream cheese mixture. Pour evenly over cake batter in a pan. Sprinkle with nuts. Bake in a preheated 350 degree oven for 35 to 45 minutes, or until cake pulls away from the sides of the pan. Cool 20 minutes. Sprinkle with some or all of the remaining sugar, as you like. Serves 16.

Co-Cola Cake

1 cup butter, softened
2 cups all-purpose flour
1³/₄ cups sugar
3 tablespoons cocoa
1 teaspoon soda
1 teaspoon vanilla
2 eggs
¹/₂ cup buttermilk
1 cup Co-cola
1¹/₂ cups miniature marshmallows

Combine all ingredients except cola and marshmallows in a large mixing bowl. Blend at low speed of mixer. Beat 1 minute at medium speed. Add cola and blend well. By hand, stir in marshmallows. Pour into a greased 13 x 9 inch pan. Bake at 325 degrees for about 40 minutes. Cool in the pan 30 minutes then ice, as follows:

¹/₂ cup soft butter
3 tablespoons cocoa
¹/₃ cup Co-Cola
4 cups confectioners' sugar

Blend until smooth and spread on cake.

Coconut Cake

1 box Duncan Hines butter cake
12 ounces frozen coconut
16 ounces sour cream
1 cup granulated sugar
4 ounces Cool Whip

Bake cake as directed in 2 8-inch pans. Cool and split into 4 layers. Mix next 3 ingredients by hand, very gently. Set aside 1 cup of this mixture for icing. Spread the balance evenly between layers, like a torte. To the cup of reserved coconut mixture, mix a 4-ounce container of Cool Whip. Ice the top and sides of cake with this. Place the cake in an airtight container for at least overnight ... preferably 48 hours. It will keep up to 4 days if kept in this container.

 # No-Crust Coconut Pie

This one's so easy, you can *fix* it while you make dinner! And it's so good while it's warm that they're going to want to eat all of it. Don't let them ... it's even better the next day!

$1/2$ cup biscuit mix
$1/2$ cup sugar
4 eggs
2 cups milk
1 cup flaked coconut
1 teaspoon vanilla extract
3 tablespoons melted butter or margarine

Combine all ingredients in the container of an electric blender. Blend on low for 1 minute. Pour mixture into a buttered 9-inch pie plate. Bake at 400 degrees for 20-25 minutes, or until pie is set.

 # Callie's Coconut Pound Cake

You know Ludlow's cousin Doodle. Well, this recipe comes from his wife, Lana. Lana's been going to a fancy cooking school downtown and learning to cook the most fabulous dishes. When I asked her for her favorite recipe, she sent this one her grandmother used for years and years. There's a moral there somewhere.

> *4 cups plain cake flour*
> *1 cup buttermilk*
> *2 cups sugar*
> *1¹/₂ cup butter*
> *1 teaspoon soda*
> *2 teaspoons cream of tartar*
> *5 eggs, separated*
> *1 cup coconut*

Beat egg whites stiff, add egg yolks. Cream butter and sugar. Add flour, soda, cream of tartar alternately with buttermilk. Add 1 cup coconut. Fold in eggs. Bake at 350 degrees for 1 hour.

Magic Cookie Bars

1 stick melted Oleo
1¹/₂ cups Graham cracker crumbs
1 cup chopped pecans
1 cup semi-sweet chocolate bits
1¹/₃ cup coconut
1 can sweetened condensed milk

Spread on a cookie sheet, in order, all the ingredients. Bake at 350 degrees for 25 minutes. Cool 15 minutes. Slice and serve.

Creme de Cacao Balls

Beverly Morgan gave these to us one Christmas in a basket filled with homemade wonderfulness. Since then, they have replaced rum balls in our house.

2¹/₂ cups crushed Oreo cookies
1 cup chopped walnuts or pecans
1 cup sifted powdered sugar
¹/₃ cup creme de cacao
2 tablespoons dark corn syrup
extra sifted powdered sugar

Mix up the crushed cookies, walnuts or pecans, and 1 cup sugar. Add creme de cacao and syrup and mix it well. Shape the dough into little 1-inch balls, and roll in powdered sugar. Put them in an airtight container and chill them overnight. It will make about 3 dozen.

 # Mama's Date Candy

2 cups sugar
1 scant cup milk
1 large piece butter
1 cup chopped dates
1 cup chopped nuts
1 teaspoon vanilla

Combine sugar, milk and butter. Let it come to a boil while stirring enough to prevent sticking. Let it boil 2 minutes. Add dates and cook rapidly until it comes to a soft boil. Remove and add nuts and vanilla. Beat until creamy. Roll in a damp cloth such as an old dinner napkin. Cut into slices before it hardens and store in a tin. It's delicious!

Dirt Cake

1 large bag Oreo cookies, crushed
¼ cup butter
1 cup confectioners' sugar
1 package (8 ounces) cream cheese
3⅓ cups milk
2 packages (3½ ounces each) French vanilla instant
*   pudding*
1 package (8 ounces) frozen whipped topping, thawed

Crush the cookies in a large plastic bag using a rolling pin, or use a food processor. Cream together the butter, confectioners' sugar and cream cheese. In another bowl, cream together the milk, instant pudding and thawed whipped topping. Combine the two mixtures. Alternate layers of the mixture and the cookie crumbs in a clean flowerpot, starting and ending with the cookie crumbs. Freeze or chill. If you want, decorate the cake with plastic flowers. Makes 10-12 servings.

 # Icebox Fruitcake

1 box Honey Graham crackers
1 box vanilla wafers
1 box seedless raisins
1 jar (15 ounces) cherries (reserve a few for garnish)
1 can (14 ounces) Eagle Brand sweetened condensed
*   milk*
1 cup pecan pieces (reserve a few for garnish)

Blend Graham crackers and vanilla wafers until you have very fine crumbs. Add all other ingredients. Mix thoroughly. Press into the shape desired and garnish with cherries and pecans. Put in refrigerator overnight.

🍴🕐🍴 Little Brandied Fruitcakes

Beverly Morgan puts these in her Christmas basket, too. You really ought to get on Beverly's Christmas list.

3 cups chopped pecans
³/₄ cup chopped candied pineapple
1¹/₂ cups quartered pitted dates
³/₄ cup halved candied cherries
³/₄ cup plain flour
³/₄ teaspoon baking powder
3 large eggs
³/₄ cup sugar
1 teaspoon vanilla
3 tablespoons brandy

Preheat oven to 300 degrees. Arrange 32 2-inch fluted foil baking cups on an ungreased cookie sheet. Put pecans and fruits in a large bowl; toss to mix. Sprinkle flour and baking powder over the top and mix with hands to coat. In another large bowl, beat eggs, sugar and vanilla until well blended. Add fruit mixture and mix with a rubber spatula until evenly blended. There will be just enough batter to cover the fruit. Fill each cup with a scant ¹/₄ cup mixture, stirring often to incorporate batter. Mixture will mound over the tops of cups. Bake 35 minutes or until pick inserted in the center comes out clean. Cool on rack. Spoon about ¼ teaspoon brandy over each cake. Store at room temperature in a covered tin up to one month.

 # Microwave Fudge

5 heaping cups powdered sugar
½ cup cocoa powder
½ cup butter
¼ cup milk
1 tablespoon vanilla
½ cup nuts

Sift powdered sugar and cocoa powder into a medium microwave-safe bowl. Cut butter into pieces and add to the bowl. Add milk. Microwave on High for 2-3 minutes or until butter is melted. Stir until mixture is smooth. Stir in vanilla and nuts. Spread in a buttered 8-inch square baking pan. Cool and cut into 64 1-inch squares.

 # Lemon Cookie Bars

1 cup flour
2 tablespoons sugar
⅛ teaspoon salt

¹/₃ stick oleo
2 eggs beaten
1 cup brown sugar
¹/₂ cup pecans
¹/₂ cup coconut
¹/₂ teaspoon vanilla
²/₃ cup confectioners' sugar
1 tablespoon lemon juice
1 teaspoon lemon rind

Mix the first four ingredients and spread on a cookie sheet. Bake at 350 degrees till lightly browned. Mix the next five ingredients and pour over the cookie layer. Bake at 350 degrees for 30 minutes and cool for 15 minutes. Mix the remaining 3 ingredients and spread over the whole thing. Cut into squares and serve.

 # Christmas Pecans

2¹/₂ cups pecans
1 cup sugar
5 tablespoons water
¹/₄ teaspoon salt
1¹/₄ teaspoons vanilla
1 teaspoon cinnamon

Toast the pecans at 300 degrees for 8 minutes. Combine all the ingredients except for the pecans and vanilla in a saucepan. Cover and slowly cook to a boil. When the mixture forms a soft ball, remove from heat. Stir in the vanilla and nuts. Pour out onto waxed paper and separate. Cool and store in covered container.

Mama's Pineapple Upside Down Cake

Buy a yellow cake mix (my mama was a very modern woman) that calls for water and egg. Use liquid from the can of pineapple (with enough water added to meet the amount of required liquid). Add the egg and beat according to the directions.

Now, melt butter in your iron skillet; half a cup should do it. Add about a half a cup of brown sugar and mix with the butter. Rub the mixture all over the sides and bottom. Place pineapple rings in the bottom of the skillet. There'll be some left. Cut those in half and place around the sides of the pan, round side up. There'll be just enough. Put a maraschino cherry in each pineapple ring hole and "half-holes."

Pour the batter into the skillet. There will probably be too much batter; throw it out. (Make sure all the pineapple is covered with batter, though.)

Bake at the temperature the package suggests. It will take longer than the directions indicate because of the iron pan. When it's brown and bounces back when you touch it, see if an inserted toothpick comes out clean.

When done, run a knife around the edge to loosen, put a platter over the skillet and turn over quickly. Let the skillet rest there for 2-3 minutes. Say a little prayer and slowly lift the skillet, leaving the cake on the platter. I hope. If some of the pineapple stays in the skillet, don't panic. Get a spatula and put it on the cake where it belongs.

Eat it warm with a glass of milk and think about your mama. I do.

Dayle's Pineapple Carrot Cake

2 cups sifted all-purpose flour
2 teaspoons baking soda
2 teaspoons ground cinnamon
1 teaspoon baking powder
1 teaspoon salt
1³/₄ cups granulated sugar
3 eggs
1 cup vegetable oil
1 teaspoon vanilla
2 cups shredded carrots
1 cup flaked coconut
1 cup coarsely chopped walnuts
1 cup crushed pineapple, drained
cream cheese frosting

Grease a 13 x 9 x 2 baking dish and dust with flour. Sift the flour, soda, baking powder, salt and cinnamon into a large bowl. Make a well in the center and add in this order: sugar, oil, eggs and vanilla. Beat with a wooden spoon until smooth. Stir in the carrots, coconut, walnuts and pineapple until well blended. Pour into the pan. Bake at 350 degrees for 45 minutes or until center springs back when touched. Cool completely on a wire rack and frost with cream cheese frosting:

Beat together 3 ounces of cream cheese and ½ stick butter; then add 2 cups sifted powdered sugar, ½ teaspoon vanilla and 2 tablespoons milk if needed to make the frosting smooth. Spread over the cake before serving.

Wonderful Bars

1 box light brown sugar
2 cups Bisquick
4 eggs, well beaten
2 cups peanuts, chopped

Combine all ingredients and pour into a greased and floured 13 x 9-inch pan. Bake at 325 degrees for 30-35 minutes. Remove from the oven and cool thoroughly before slicing. May be dusted with powdered sugar before serving if desired.

Ludlow's Irish Coffee

Put a moderate (?) slug of Bushmill's Irish Whiskey in a cup. Add a tablespoon of brown sugar. Fill the cup with hot coffee and stir. Top with frozen whipped topping that is still frozen (tastes like lite ice cream). Garnish with a cherry. On your second cup, leave off the cherry. On your third cup, the whipped topping. In the fourth, the sugar. In the fifth, omit that damn coffee ... And, after the sixth cup ... go buy a seeing-eye dog!

THE WHACKOS' RECIPES

The whackos are the most creative, wonderful people on earth. I have been referring to the folks who call me on my radio show "Whackos" for about 20 years. They come in all ages, races, shapes and sizes. They are the Best! If the following Whacko recipes are not all wonderful, I will publically pull out my eyebrows.

Kitty Litter's Black Beans in White Wine

Kitty's black beans are the best anywhere. Served with her slaw and Cuban bread — Wow!

> *1 pound black beans*
> *¼ pound salt pork cut in 4 pieces*
> *2 celery ribs, including leaves, chopped*
> *1 carrot, chopped*
> *1 onion stuck with 2 cloves*
> *2 cloves garlic*
> *1 big dried chili pepper*
> *1 bay leaf*
> *1 cup white wine (chablis blanc)*
> *1 teaspoon thyme*
> *1 teaspoon salt*
> *½ teaspoon ground pepper*
> *2 tablespoons chopped parsley*

Wash, pick, and soak beans. Drain and put in pot with four quarts water and salt pork. Tie next 6 ingredients in cheesecloth and add to the pot. Simmer for 45 minutes, or until the beans are just tender. Discard salt pork and cheesecloth bag. Drain the beans but save the liquid.

Put beans in large casserole, add wine, 1 cup of bean liquid, thyme, salt and pepper. Cover and bake at 350 for 2 hours stirring 2 or 3 times. Add more liquid if they seem dry. Stir in parsley and serve with sour cream and chopped sweet onions on the side.

Lofty A-Frame's Paté de Campagne

I don't know if you're into paté or not, but you owe it to yourself to try this. It's hard to describe this to somebody who is not really a paté eater. Give it a try anyway. It's sort of a rich man's potted meat. (—Ludlow)

> *1 pound ground veal or pork*
> *1 pound beef liver, ground*
> *2 shallots, finely chopped*
> *¹/₂ pound ham, coarsely chopped*
> *1 carrot, chopped finely*
> *2 tablespoons fine herbs*
> *2 tablespoons Asbach Uralt or other fine brandy*
> *1 clove crushed garlic*
> *1 teaspoon black pepper and salt*
> *bacon*
> *bay leaves*

Mix ground meats, shallots, carrot, herbs, brandy, garlic, and salt and pepper together in a bowl. Line the sides of a terrine with bacon and spoon mixture into the terrine. Press mixture into the terrine and decorate the top of the mixture with bay leaves. Cover and bake in a 350 degree oven for about an hour and one-half or until the paté is firm to the touch. Serve with pearl onions, grainy mustard, sweet gherkins, butter, and crusty French bread.

Freckles' Bits of Heaven

2 cups self-rising flour
2 sticks butter, melted
8 ounces sour cream
1 cup sharp cheese, shredded

Mix together and bake in muffin tins for 30 minutes at 350 degrees. This is so easy, but it will make you slap your pappy. I've seen grown women fight over the last one!

 # Lee's Ham Delights

3 packages Tatum rolls, or Pepperidge Farm dinner
   rolls
3 teaspoons Worcestershire sauce
3 tablespoons mustard
1 medium onion, chopped
3 tablespoons poppy seeds
½ pound margarine
1 pound boiled ham
¾ pound Swiss cheese, sliced

Slice rolls in the middle, separating top and bottom. Cream the margarine and add onion, mustard, and all seasonings. Stir in poppy seeds. Spread this mixture on the top and bottom of the rolls. Add ham and cheese and wrap in foil. Bake at 400 degrees for 10 minutes. Cut into individual servings.

Madame Zero's Holo-E-Good Spread

Swiss cheese, grated
purple onion, grated
mayonnaise

Just blend all ingredients to taste and spread on rye crackers.

Sally's Pork Tenderloin Surprise Package

For each serving:
3 strips bacon, thick
1 center-cut boneless pork chop, butterflied (³/₄ inch
thick)
1 slice Vidalia onion
1 slice bell pepper
1 slice tomato

Criss cross the bacon slices. Lay the pork in the middle and salt and pepper. Stack onion, green pepper and tomato on top. Wrap the bacon slices up around the entire stack and secure it with two or three toothpicks. Place on grill with a drip pan under. Use a covered BBQ kettle and cook indirect method on low heat for 1 hour. Place a slice of cheese, any kind you like, on top and let it melt on each. This takes about 3-5 minutes. Take out the toothpicks and serve.

Roxanne's Cuban Sandwich

1 loaf French bread
dill pickle chips
yellow mustard
butter or margarine
6 ounces smoked turkey, sliced thin
6 ounces boiled ham, sliced thin
6 ounces Swiss cheese, sliced thin

Spread one side of split French bread with mustard. Spread butter or margarine on the other side. Lay out all pieces of turkey, cheese and ham on the bread and top with a row of dill pickle slices. Cut bread in half. In a large skillet, set one half of the sandwich buttered lightly top and bottom. Place a heavy iron or something to press the sandwich almost flat; do this on both sides. Serve hot.

Polly Ester's Zucchini, Potato and Cheese Casserole

3 medium zucchini thinly sliced (about 1 pound)
3 medium potatoes, peeled and sliced
2 cups grated Monterey Jack cheese
1 cup stuffing mix or bread crumbs
1/2 cup chopped parsley

garlic powder
3 tablespoons olive oil
3 tablespoons butter
salt and pepper
¼ cup water

Butter a 1½-quart casserole and layer ⅓ of the zucchini and potato slices. Put ⅓ of the cheese, stuffing and parsley on top of the vegetable slices. Sprinkle with salt, pepper and garlic to taste and drizzle with one tablespoon of the olive oil. Repeat each layer twice, drizzling each with oil. Dot the top with butter and pour water over all. Cover and bake at 350 degrees for 1 hour.

 # Sara's Potatoes Deluxe

2 pounds frozen hash brown potatoes
1 cup diced onions
1 cup cream of chicken soup
1 pound sour cream
1 stick margarine
8 ounces sharp Cheddar cheese, grated
2 cups corn flakes

Thaw potatoes about 30 minutes. Combine onions, cheese, soup and sour cream. Mix with potatoes and salt and pepper to taste. Top with 2 cups of corn flakes blended with ½ cup melted margarine. Bake 1 hour at 350 degrees.

Edna's Chitterlings

Boil clean chitterlings in salted water for 3 hours. Batter and fry in deep fat. Dip in mustard sauce or barbeque sauce.

(There is no way to fix chitterlings where they are fit to eat. Folks have been trying to get me to like these horrors all my life. I would rather eat a Motorola radio. — Ludlow)

 # Ciero's Grilled Peanut Butter and Jelly Sandwich

Make a peanut butter and jelly sandwich. Put butter on the outside and grill it like a grilled cheese sandwich.

This must be eaten with a fork (or naked, sitting in a bathtub).

Serve with a large glass of ice cold, sweet milk.

Dee Tour's
Easy Cheese Ball

2 packages cream cheese (8 ounces)
1 jar chipped beef, chopped
¹/₂ cup chopped pecans
1 tablespoon dried onion

Combine softened cream cheese, onion and chipped beef. Roll into chopped pecans.

Charles DeGaulle's
Pumpkin Casserole

1 pumpkin, about 12 inches in diameter
2 pounds ground beef, slightly browned
3 cups Irish potatoes, diced and cooked nearly done
2 cups onions
1 cup celery

Prepare pumpkin by cutting out stem, leaving hole 3 to 4 inches in diameter. Save top. Clean out seeds and all strings. Salt and pepper inside, then turn upside down to drain overnight (or several hours).

Add vegetables to ground beef, mixing thoroughly. Pack the mixture into the pumpkin, place stem back in place, put in a pan and cook at 350 degrees for about 1 to 1¹/₂ hours, or until the pumpkin is soft.

Silly Sally's Ragu-Stuffed Chicken Breasts

10 ounces Swiss cheese, diced
2 eggs, lightly beaten
3 tablespoons seasoned bread crumbs
3 tablespoons chopped fresh parsley
1/4 teaspoon salt
1/8 teaspoon pepper
pinch of nutmeg
6 large boneless chicken breasts, pounded thin
2 tablespoons olive or vegetable oil
2 cups Ragu garden-style spaghetti sauce with green
  peppers and mushrooms.

In a medium bowl, thoroughly combine cheese, eggs, bread crumbs, parsley, salt, pepper and nutmeg. Place 1/4 cup of the cheese mixture in the center of each chicken breast. Roll and secure with toothpicks. In a large skillet, heat the oil and thoroughly brown the chicken on all sides. Drain the fat. Pour spaghetti sauce over chicken breasts and simmer, covered for 45 minutes or till done.

 # Roger's Goulash

1 pound ground meat, browned
3-4 carrots, sliced thin
1 onion sliced thin
1/4 cup raw rice
1 can tomatoes, chopped

Put half of the browned meat into a casserole and put a layer of carrots, rice and onions. Repeat the layers until all the ingredients are used up. Pour tomatoes over all. If it looks like there isn't enough juice, add 1 small can of tomato juice. Cover and bake 1-1½ hours at 350 degrees.

Big Yellow Bird's Fried Vegetable Supreme

1 cup self-rising flour
1 tablespoon salt
1 teaspoon pepper
1 cup milk
1 tablespoon cooking oil
1 tablespoon paprika
1 egg
any vegetables, sliced
Parmesan cheese, grated
enough oil to cover vegetables when frying

Combine the first 7 ingredients, and blend to the consistency of pancake batter. Heat the oil in the deep fryer. Dip vegetables in the batter and fry until brown. Drain on paper towels. Sprinkle with Parmesan cheese. This is especially delicious with zucchini, square green tomatoes and Vidalia onions.

Mama-of-Barnesville's Vidalia Onion Pie

1¹/₂ cups soda cracker crumbs
¹/₂ cup melted butter
2¹/₂ cups thinly sliced raw Vidalia onions
2 tablespoons butter
1 cup milk
3 eggs, slightly beaten
¹/₂ pound grated Cheddar cheese

Mix crumbs with melted butter and press into a 10-inch pie pan. Saute the onions in the 2 tablespoons butter and pour into the crust. Scald the milk and add slowly into the eggs. Add grated cheese and stir till cheese melts. Pour over onions and bake at 350 degrees for 45 minutes.

Ray's C.L.O.T. Sandwich

Chitterlings (pronounced chittlins)
lettuce
onion
tomato
white bread
mayonnaise

Ray says, "You take it from here."

Winsome, Losesome's Chess Pie

1/2 pound butter
1/2 cup sugar
3 eggs
1 teaspoon vinegar
1 teaspoon vanilla

Melt the butter and add the sugar, eggs, vinegar and vanilla. Cook in a 400 degree oven till the edges turn brown. Turn off the heat and let the pie stay in the oven until it sets.

Gwen Ray's Pecan Pinto Bean Pie

"A delight to the palate," Gwen promises.

1 cup cooked pinto beans
1 small can coconut
3 cups sugar
2 sticks margarine, melted
4 eggs
1 cup chopped pecans
1 tablespoon vanilla
3 9-inch unbaked pie shells

Mash beans well. In a large mixing bowl, beat eggs until slightly thickened. Fold in remaining ingredients and mix well. Pour into 3 unbaked pie shells. Bake in a preheated 300 degree oven for 45 minutes. Baked pies can be frozen for use later.

 # Maw Maw's Famous Banana Nut Bread

¹/₂ cup cooking oil
1 cup sugar
2 eggs
1 teaspoon vanilla
2-3 very ripe bananas, mashed
2 cups self-rising flour, sifted
¹/₂ cup chopped pecans

Mix together the oil, sugar, eggs and vanilla. Add the bananas and mix well. Add the flour and combine thoroughly. Stir in the pecans. Pour the batter into a greased and floured loaf pan. Bake at 350 degrees till done and golden brown. Cool 10-15 minutes before removing from the pan.

Bloody Mary's Cream Cheese Pound Cake

1 cup margarine, softened
¹/₂ cup butter, softened (do not substitute)
1 8-ounce package cream cheese, softened
3 cups sugar
6 eggs
3 cups sifted cake flour
2 teaspoons vanilla extract

Combine the first three ingredients and beat well with a heavy-duty mixer. Gradually add sugar, beat until light and fluffy (about 5 minutes). Add eggs, one at a time; beat well after each addition. Add flour to creamed mixture and beat well. Stir in vanilla. Pour the batter into a well greased 10-inch tube pan. Bake at 325 degrees for 1 hour and 30 minutes or until cake tests done. Cool in the pan for 10 minutes. Remove from pan and cool completely.

Sandy's Poppy Seed Cake

1 package Duncan Hines deluxe yellow cake mix
1 package (3³/₄ ounces) French Vanilla pudding mix,
    instant
4 eggs
1 cup sour cream
¹/₂ cup Crisco oil
¹/₂ cup cream sherry
¹/₂ cup poppy seeds

Combine all ingredients, stirring to blend. Beat at medium speed for 5 minutes, scraping the sides of the bowl frequently. Pour into a greased and floured bundt or tube pan. Bake at 325 degrees for 50 minutes to 1 hour. Cool in the pan for 15 minutes, then turn out onto a plate. Cool completely before cutting.

 # Cheryl's Coconut Pudding with Raspberry Sauce

1 cup sugar
1 envelope gelatin
¹/₂ teaspoon salt
1¹/₄ cups milk
1 teaspoon vanilla
1 3¹/₂ ounce can flaked coconut
2 cups heavy cream, whipped

Combine the sugar, gelatin, salt and milk over medium heat in a sauce pan until sugar and gelatin are dissolved. Chill until partially set. Add vanilla. Fold in coconut and whipped cream. Pour into a 6-cup mold and refrigerate until set. When ready to serve, unmold on a plate and serve with raspberry sauce, as follows:

1 10-ounce package frozen raspberries
1¹/₂ teaspoon cornstarch
¹/₂ cup red currant jelly

Combine all ingredients in a saucepan over medium heat. Bring to a boil, strain through a sieve and chill.

Grace's Red Gold Jam

4 cups chopped tomatoes
4 cups sugar
2 tablespoons lemon juice
1 6-ounce strawberry jello

Combine tomatoes, sugar and lemon juice, bring to a boil and simmer for 20 minutes, stirring frequently. Remove from heat and add jello, stir until completely dissolved. Pour into sterilized jars and store in refrigerator. This is a beautiful jam that will keep for quite a long time.

 # Choo Choo Man's Dill Pickles

Use small cucumbers. Wash them well. Rinse jars in hot water. Place cucumbers in jars and pour hot water over them. Mix 2 quarts water, 1 quart vinegar, ½ cup plain salt and bring the mixture to a boil. Stir well. Pour the water out of the jars. Put one teaspoon dill seed over the cucumbers in jars. Pour the liquid mixture over the cucumbers and put one slice of onion in each. Seal well for 1 week. Pickles are ready to eat.

Miller Pope's
Steak & Vegetable Wok

Miller Pope's no whacko. He's no ordinary cook either. He's a very tall cook.

He's also the world's tallest radio producer.

I liked Miller the first time I met him. I found out that his full name is Miller Harris Pope. I ask you, how Southern can you get? Three last names! That makes him more southern than bullet holes in a road sign.

It also means he can cook like a son of a gun. (—Ludlow)

¹/₂ cup onions, yellow or Vidalia, chopped
¹/₂ cup sliced fresh mushrooms
¹/₂ cup sliced carrots
¹/₂ cup sliced yellow squash
¹/₂ cup sliced zucchini
¹/₂ cup green beans cut into small pieces
¹/₄ cup snow peas
small handful fresh beans sprouts
6 ounces round steak
³/₄ cup soy sauce
1 teaspoon sesame oil

Cut steak into thin strips and then cut strips in half. Marinate in soy sauce for at least one hour. Heat wok for 2-3 minutes without oil. Add one teaspoon peanut oil and immediately add the steak. Don't use but a little of the soy sauce in the wok. When the steak is just browned, remove and set aside. Add onions to the wok and stir till just clear. Add steak back and all other vegetables. Cook, stirring frequently till vegetables are tender crisp. Add sesame oil and toss just before serving over cooked white rice. Serves 4, or 2 with my appetite.

Miller's Classic South Georgia Sandwich

*2 pieces of bread, white of course (can be lightly
    toasted or used straight from the bag)*
chunky peanut butter
Kraft real mayonnaise
*1 thick slice of Vidalia onion (Texas sweet onions can
    be substituted, if you have to, but they have to be
    thinly sliced)*

Spread a thick layer of peanut butter on one slice of bread.
Spread a thin layer of mayonnaise on the other slice of bread.
Place the onion in the middle of the mayonnaise slice so that
the edges of the onion touch the crust of the bread. Place the
peanut butter slice on top of the onion and mash gently to
mix the mayonnaise and the peanut butter. This is best when
served with an *ice*-cold glass of milk.

 # Miller's Easy Creamed Corn

8 ears shucked corn
*corn creamer (this device can be found at most
    hardware stores or kitchen specialty shops)*
1 stick butter
iron skillet or frying pan

The corn creamer makes this easier and better than just
cutting the corn off with a knife. Put a large bowl under the

corn creamer. Use a little elbow grease to clean every kernel off the ear. After the kernels are off, keep creaming to get every bit of "corn milk" off the ear. You may break a sweat, but the end result is well worth it.

Melt the butter in the skillet. Add the corn and stir well over low heat for 15-20 minutes. Remember, the corn sticks quickly so keep an eye on it. Stirring will prevent the sticking.

A serving suggestion: Pour the corn over a fresh opened biscuit with a thin slice of onion on top.

SAUCES

Spaghetti Sauce

Saute ½ pound mushrooms, covered until they lose about half their moisture. Set aside. Saute a chopped onion and a minced garlic clove in your iron skillet until the onion is translucent. Add 1-1½ pounds lean ground beef, broken up. Add a little salt. Cover the skillet and cook till the meat is done, but not browned. Drain well. Add:

> *1 medium can tomato sauce*
> *1 medium can stewed tomatoes*
> *1 little can tomato paste*
> *¼ cup Worcestershire sauce (Lee & Perrins)*
> *1 tablespoon oregano*
> *1 teaspoon celery seed*
> *2-4 drops Tabasco*

Simmer a few minutes. Taste and adjust the seasonings. (Lud's "tasting" involves slathering the sauce on a piece of white bread, folding it over, eating and groaning with ecstasy.)

 # Horseradish Sauce

This is a great sauce, but if you get too much horseradish in it, it could kill you. (— Ludlow)

> *½ cup mayonnaise*
> *½ cup horseradish*
> *2 tablespoons Dijon mustard*
> *1 teaspoon sugar*

Mix and refrigerate.

Pot Likker

Pot likker is the liquid left from cooking turnip greens. The idea is to pour it in a bowl, crumble cornbread in it, and eat it.

I suppose if you're hungry enough, and out of buttermilk . . . naa.

(I can just see it now . . . hundreds of my northern brethren reading this and saying, "Oooooo . . . pot likker . . . that sounds gross." To these folks, I would just say, "Hush and eat it . . . it's wonderful." — Ludlow)

Ludlow's Red-eye Gravy

After you fry country ham and take it out of the skillet, there's grease and brown stuff stuck to the pan. Leave it all just as it is and pour in coffee. Stir and scrape the pan as you heat it. When the skillet is as clean as it's gonna get and the gravy is hot, pour it into the bowl and serve it over cat-head biscuits.

Sopping is permitted.

If you don't have any biscuits, don't bother with this.

EAT THIS, YOU'LL FEEL BETTER

The fact of the matter is: if you're sick, you don't want to eat. If you're sick at my house, you're, by God, going to eat. You may die, but you're going to have something in your belly when you do.

Science has finally admitted that chicken soup has curative powers. We all knew that.

And bananas will flat fix the large intestine — either by getting things moving along, or slowing them down.

So, no excuses, eat this, you'll feel better.

Chicken Broth

Because you've read this book, you have chicken stock in your refrigerator. Make sure you've lifted the fat off the top before you use it for medicinal purposes. Even the sickest person can tolerate chicken broth.

As the patient improves, add bits of pasta, chicken and vegetables. Pretty soon, he'll be back on his feet.

 # The Milkshake

1 scoop vanilla ice cream
1½ cups of milk
½ banana
1 raw egg
dash of cinnamon
tad sugar or honey

Mix it all together in a blender.

When the patient has rebelled about all the chicken soup (it worked if he's well enough to rebel), go to the milkshake. Sometimes flu victims choose to live off this. (Never *ever* tell the patient about the raw egg—the knowledge can cause severe retching.)

A Cup of Tea

The caffeine in the tea makes the patient think he feels better than he actually does. Add a spoonful of sugar and he'll have some energy. Add a slug of whiskey and he's well.

Tomato Soup

Use canned tomato soup—you've got enough to do with sickness in the house—dilute it with milk.

Soda Crackers and Ginger Ale

As horrible as it sounds, this is all some folks will eat when they're sick. It's what my mama gave me and I'm still here.

Winter Day Soup

1 can chicken broth
1 can V8 juice
1 beef bouillion cube
chopped parsley
juice of ½ lemon

Mix and heat through.

 # Milk Toast

Milk toast is horrible. You heat milk, toast bread, put the milk in a bowl, put the toast on top and sprinkle the mess with sugar and cinnamon.

The only person I know who was forced to eat this concoction as a child is now prematurely gray. There is no scientific data concerning this phenomenon, but I'd never give milk toast to a child of mine.

(One time, my friend Lardo's mother tried to make him eat milk toast. He killed her, and the jury turned him loose. — Ludlow)

POTPOURRI

Chicken Stock

I make chicken stock as soon as I come home from the grocery store, before I've put anything up.

As I unload the groceries, I put all the vegetables on the counter by the sink and get out my big pot with a lid.

I take the papery peels off the onions and garlic and put them in the pot. Then I scrub the carrots and peel them, and put the peelings in the pot. All of the ugly stalks of celery and the parts I don't plan to use go in the pot. Even the tough brown ends of the mushrooms go in.

I rewrap the clean vegetables and put them in the refrigerator.

Next I take the fresh chicken parts and wash them. I skin the chicken and debone it if I want fillets. The skin and bones go in the pot.

I cover this "garbage" with water, add some salt, put the lid on it and let it boil while I get the groceries put away. After 30 to 45 minutes I put the lid in the dishwasher and let the stock boil until the amount of liquid is reduced by about half.

Finally I strain the liquid into Mason jars and throw away the solids. I use it all week for sauces and gravies; to cook rice or potatoes in; to make soup or dressing with, or to use for medicinal purposes.

(Unless I plan to use the chicken fat for chicken gravy, I lift the fat off the top when the stock is cold. Our tongues don't mind and our arteries appreciate it.)

Ludlow's Peanuts in a Co-Cola

In order to really enjoy peanuts in a Co-Cola it's necessary that you have them in a country store somewhere in the deep South. Once inside the store, find the drink box, reach down in that freezing cold water, and feel around until you find the unmistakable shape of a six-ounce Co-Cola. (In certain backward sections of America it's pronounced Coca-Cola.)

(I cannot over-emphasize that no other soft drink will work with this recipe. Once, many years ago, a man in Eugene, Oregon, named John Richard Morse used a Pepsi Cola. Legend has it that for the rest of his life, he was plagued by severe cramps in his great toe. IT'S JUST TOO BIG A CHANCE TO TAKE!)

Once you've opened the Co-Cola, look around the store until you find the penny peanut machine. You remember, the one with the glass globe, full to the brim with those red, salted Spanish peanuts. No other kind of peanut will do. You'll need at least two cents worth, although three cents worth would be better.

Before you put the nuts in the bottle, take a big drink; this will allow room enough for the peanuts. Add the nuts and enjoy this mid-afternoon treat. When all the drink is gone you will still have three peanuts stuck to the bottom of the bottle.

To get the last few nuts, hold the bottle in your left hand, put the bottle to your lips, and raise the bottle until it's pointing straight up. Take your right hand and gently tap the bottom of the bottle until the peanuts fall in your mouth.

Put the empty bottle in the wooden crate next to the drink box, give the man a nickel for the drink, go outside and get on your bike and ride home.

Deviled Eggs

I think my mother's deviled eggs were like every mother's deviled eggs:

> *egg yolk*
> *mayonnaise*
> *mustard*
> *pickle relish*
> *salt & pepper*

She just mashed it all, put it back in the egg white, and sprinkled with paprika.

Marlene Sanders does something different. She mashes the yolk with mayonnaise, salt and pepper and garlic powder, stuffs it in the egg white and tops it with the thinnest slice of stuffed olive. It tastes so *adult* and the flavor isn't confused with the potato salad (that I make with mustard, mayonnaise and pickle relish).

 # Charlie's Popcorn

Our youngest, Charlie, makes fantastic popcorn. He's been doing it since he was in grammar school.

He buys expensive popcorn and pops it in a popcorn popper, then the creative genius comes out. Sometimes he mixes butter and Tabasco to pour on it, or sprinkles garlic salt on it. Chili powder isn't bad. The dried cheese stuff out of packaged macaroni and cheese is good. Or onion salt.

It never occurred to me to fool with popcorn until Charlie started.

So experiment! It's fun.

 # Freezer Pickles

12 cucumbers, unpeeled, thinly sliced
2 Vidalia onions, thinly sliced
1/4 cup salt
4-6 cups sugar
1 quart cider vinegar
1 teaspoon celery seed

Layer cucumber and onion slices in a large earthenware bowl. Sprinkle with salt and cover with two trays of ice cubes. Let stand at room temperature for about 2 hours, then drain off the water. In enamel pot, bring sugar, vinegar and celery seed to a boil, then let the mixture cool slightly. Pack cucumber and onion slices into each pint container (square plastic containers work well). Pour hot syrup into each container leaving an inch head-space. When completely cool, cover and freeze. Makes about 6 pints. To use the pickles, thaw for 24 hours in refrigerator.

Teenie's Pepper Relish

12 red peppers
12 green peppers
12 onions
2 cups sugar
2 cups vinegar
3 tablespoons salt

Chop peppers and onions. Cover with boiling water and let them stand for 5 minutes. Drain. Add vinegar, sugar and salt and boil the mixture for 5 minutes. Pour into clean, hot jars and seal immediately.

Diane's Ten Best Cooking Hints

1. Make chicken stock every time you buy chicken.

2. The box says to pour the boiling water into the Jell-O. Don't. Pour the Jell-O into the boiling water and let it come back to a boil. It will gel every time.

3. If you're using instant coffee, put the coffee into the boiling water and let it boil for a second or two. It won't taste quite so "instant."

4. Flirt with your butcher.

5. To peel a raw tomato, dip it in boiling water for one minute. The peeling will slide off. (Connie Pope says to rub the tomato all over with the dull side of the blade and it will do the same thing.)

6. Put a strand of spaghetti on the tines of a fork. Hold the fork in your left fist with your thumb on the back of the handle. With your right index finger pull down on the tines and flip the strand against the wall. If it sticks, it's done. (Or you could taste it.)

7. Spring for an electric knife sharpener. Charlie gave me one for Mother's day and changed my life.

8. To peel boiled eggs easily, as soon as the timer goes off, pour off the hot water and shake the pan hard to break all the shells. Immediately fill the pot with ice and water and go away. After 10 to 15 minutes they'll slide right out of the shells. (If you like to eat them hot, you're on your own.)

9. Buy bread flour for breads. Buy cake flour for cakes. Those flour people know what they're about.

10. If your spouse comes up behind you while you're cooking and woo-woo's your neck, turn off the stove and woo-woo him right back. In the great scheme of things, cookin' don't matter, lovin' do.

INDEX

NOTES

NOTES

NOTES

NOTES

NOTES

NOTES